# LIGHTING

CHRIS WESTON

**An AVA Book**
Published by AVA Publishing SA
Rue des Fontenailles 16
Case Postale
1000 Lausanne 6
Switzerland
Tel: +41 786 005 109
Email: enquiries@avabooks.ch

Distributed by Thames & Hudson (ex-North America)
181a High Holborn
London WC1V 7QX
United Kingdom
Tel: +44 20 7845 5000
Fax: +44 20 7845 5055
Email: sales@thameshudson.co.uk
www.thamesandhudson.com

Distributed by Sterling Publishing Co., Inc.
in the USA
387 Park Avenue South
New York, NY 10016-8810
Tel: +1 212 532 7160
Fax: +1 212 213 2495
www.sterlingpub.com

in Canada
Sterling Publishing
c/o Canadian Manda Group
One Atlantic Avenue, Suite 105
Toronto, Ontario M6K 3E7

English Language Support Office
AVA Publishing (UK) Ltd.
Tel: +44 1903 204 455
Email: enquiries@avabooks.co.uk



ISBN 2-88479-101-9 and 978-2-88479-101-4

10 9 8 7 6 5 4 3 2 1

Production by AVA Book Production Pte. Ltd., Singapore
Tel: +65 6334 8173
Fax: +65 6259 9830
Email: production@avabooks.com.sg

# HOW TO GET THE MOST FROM THIS BOOK

This book introduces different aspects of photographic lighting via dedicated sections for each topic. The text offers a straightforward guide to the most frequently asked questions alongside photographic examples and technical diagrams.

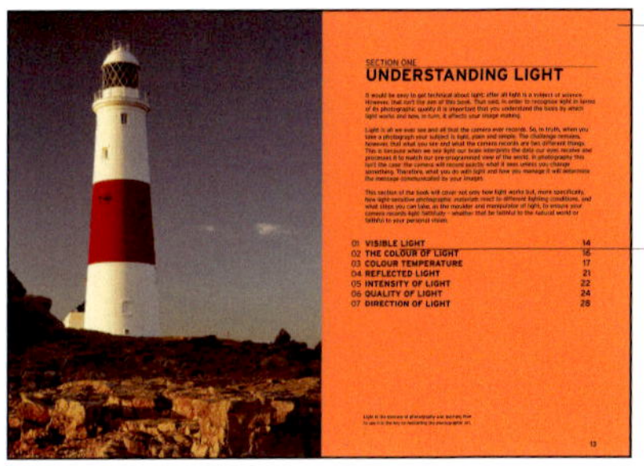


**Sections**
This book is divided into eight sections, each one exploring a different aspect of lighting. The sections are identified by a different colour. The opening pages of each section clearly display the colour for that chapter.

**Topics**
The topics in each dedicated section are all listed on the subject introduction page.

**Colour-coded tabs**
Colour-coded tabs appear in the corner of each page to identify the section.

**Clear navigation**
Each of the 50 topics is numbered in the top corner of the page to make them easy to find.

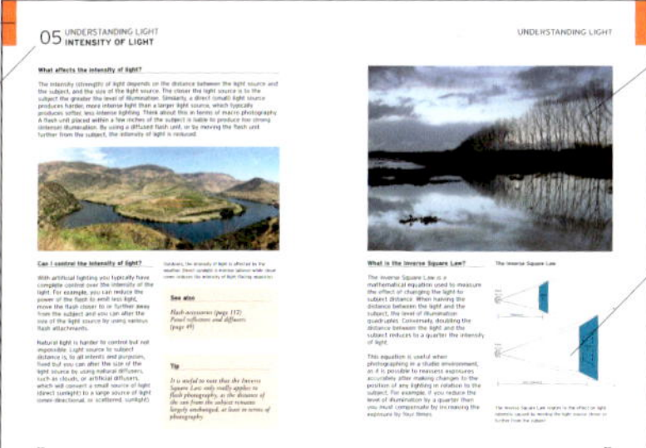


**Visual explanations**
Each question is illustrated using a series of photographic examples.

**Diagrams**
Additional technical information is provided and explained by the use of simple diagrams and icons.

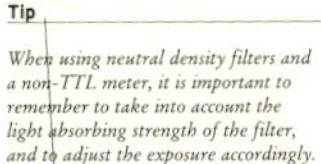


**Tips**
Look out for these panels, which offer handy tips on a variety of topics.

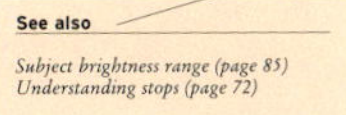


**FAQs**
A complete list of all the FAQs appears alongside the subject index.

**See also**
See also boxes cross-reference a topic to other related questions or topics that appear in the book.

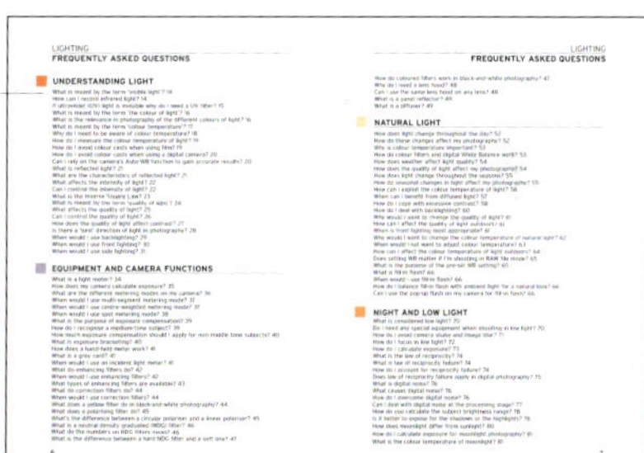


## Icon key

A simple reference guide to the symbols used within the diagrams.

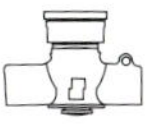 Camera

 Light direction

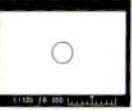 Viewfinder

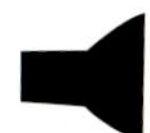 Flash

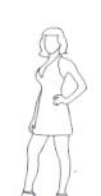 Subject

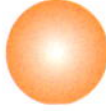 Light source

PHOTOGRAPHY FAQS

# LIGHTING

LIGHTING

# FREQUENTLY ASKED QUESTIONS

## UNDERSTANDING LIGHT



## EQUIPMENT AND CAMERA FUNCTIONS

## NATURAL LIGHT



## NIGHT AND LOW LIGHT

# FREQUENTLY ASKED QUESTIONS

## CLOSE-UP AND MACRO PHOTOGRAPHY



## THE DAYLIGHT STUDIO



## ARTIFICIAL LIGHT

## ARTIFICIAL STUDIO LIGHTING

# INTRODUCTION

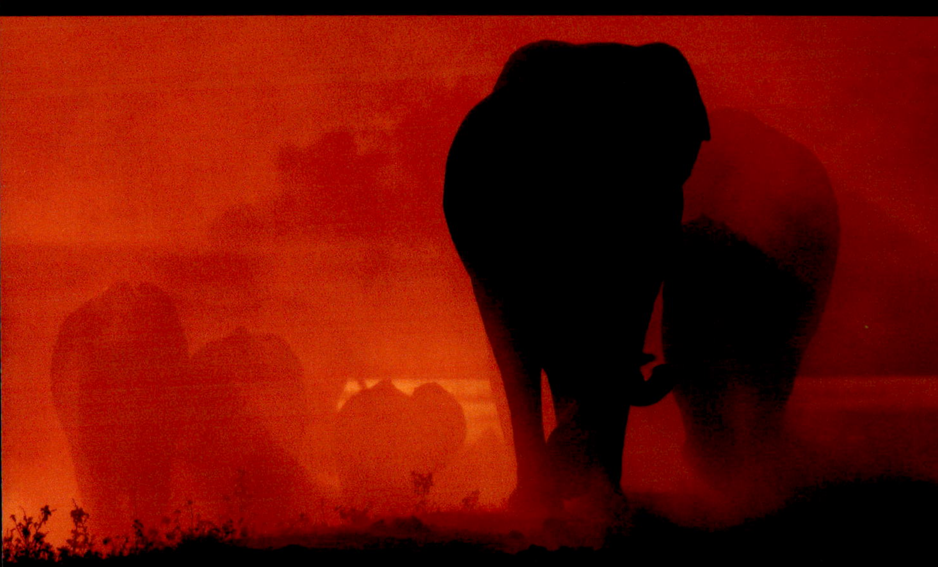

Photographers use and manipulate light to define their own impression of a scene. There is no right or wrong way to capture light, simply one person's visual opinion, or statement, about a moment in time.

Light is the photographer's primary tool. Without it there would be no photographs. Yet it is quite amazing to me how many would-be photographers take light for granted or believe there is only one way to light a subject. As an example, let me relate to you a story. I was taking photographs of a castle in England and had been for most of the days of that past week.

This particular morning a young chap happened along, set up his tripod and, within a few minutes, had fired half a dozen shots and packed away his gear. Just before he set off he turned to me and said: 'Well, that's the castle done.' I can't remember my exact reaction but I think I simply nodded in dumbfounded surprise and reapplied my attention to my own camera.

I took several photographs of the castle that day, indeed that week, and not one of them looks the same. In each the light is different, giving every picture a unique atmosphere and a different story to tell. For what each of those pictures says is, this is what this castle looked like on this particular day, at this particular time and under these particular weather conditions. If I were to go back tomorrow, no doubt I would find a different tale to be told - and this is the wonder of photography.

How we illustrate these tales of mystery and adventure, wonder and awe, dark foreboding and bright opportunity is through our interpretation and manipulation of light. Light gives your pictures character. It transforms them from two-dimensional pictures on pieces of paper to three-dimensional, living images that embody not only the scene you saw with your eyes but also your personal interpretation of that scene, moulded by a lifetime of experiences and emotional reactions, of prejudices and desires. Without an ability to control light you will never be able to consistently stamp your photographs with your own imprint and they will rarely live up to your expectations.

So, learning how to use light to the very edges of its potential is a fundamental requirement if you are to step beyond the confinements of technical mediocrity and set yourself apart from the photographic also-rans. The fact that you have read this far is enough to tell me that you want to learn; that you want your pictures to say something different about you. In essence you want your photographs to have that something special that we in the game call the WOW factor.
So, thank you for sticking with me this far and I hope you find in the following pages the answers to all the questions you have about photographic lighting.

Sometimes light is the obvious subject of an image, such as with this picture of fireworks. However, in reality, light is all we ever capture with our cameras and understanding its nuances and how to work with light are critical to successful photography.

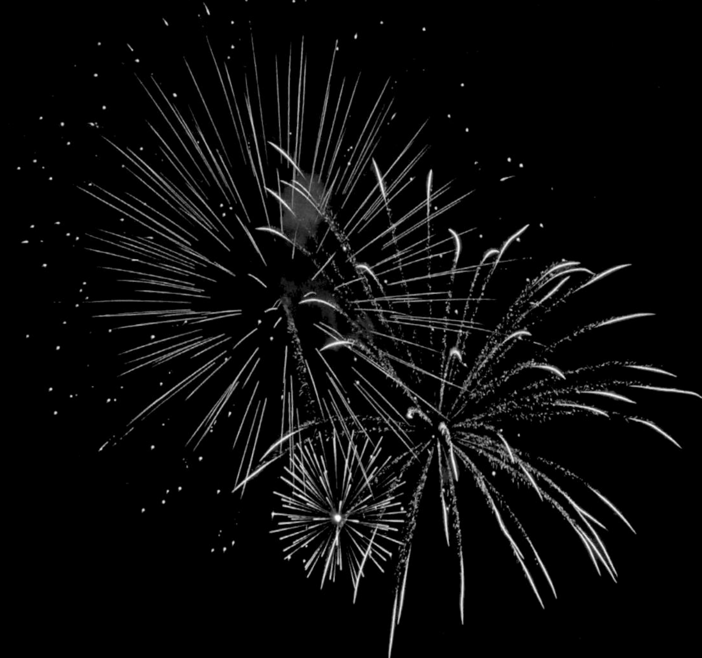

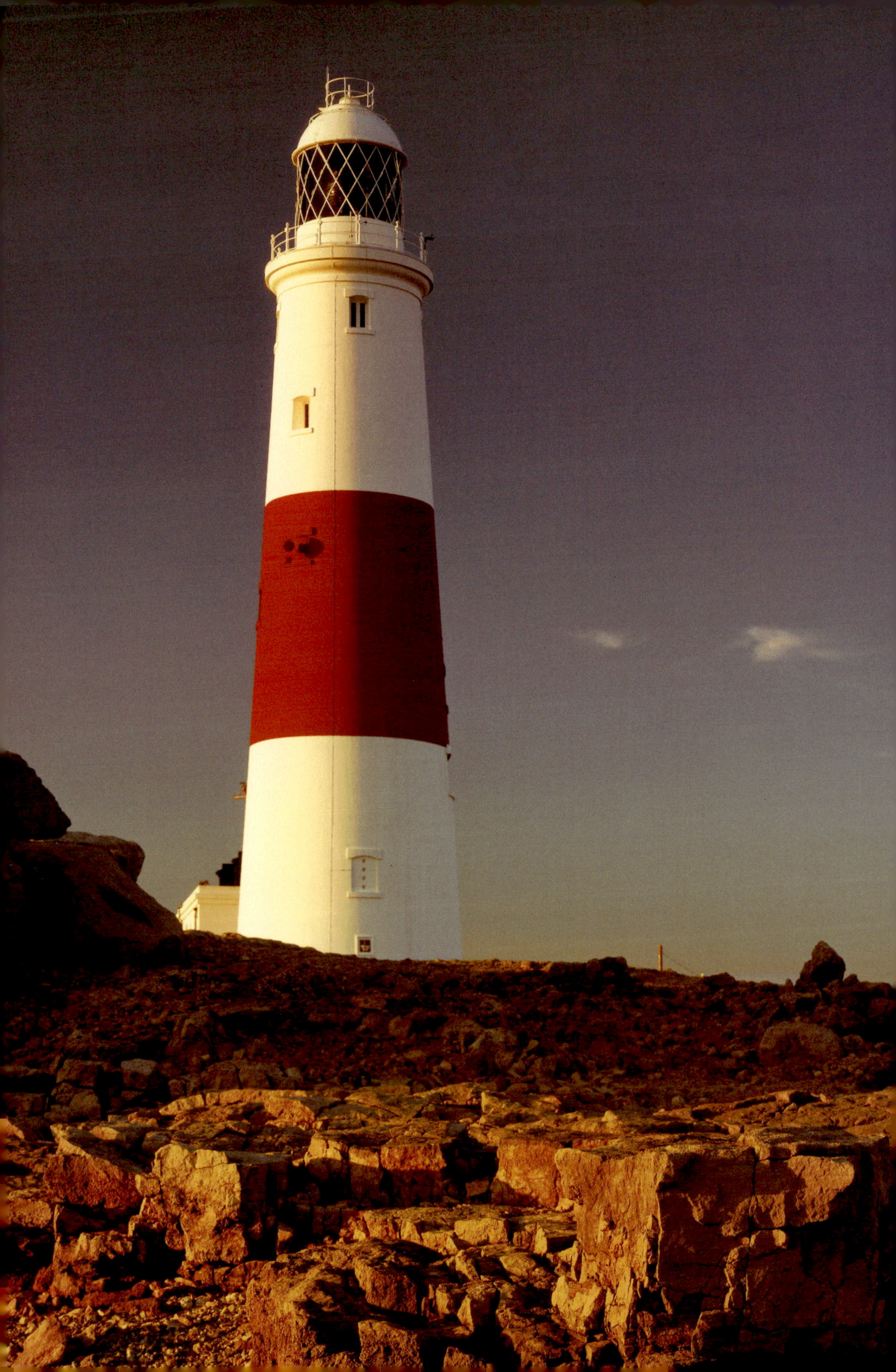

SECTION ONE

# UNDERSTANDING LIGHT

It would be easy to get technical about light; after all light is a subject of science. However, that isn't the aim of this book. That said, in order to recognise light in terms of its photographic quality it is important that you understand the basis by which light works and how, in turn, it affects your image making.

Light is all we ever see and all that the camera ever records. So, in truth, when you take a photograph your subject is light, plain and simple. The challenge remains, however, that what you see and what the camera records are two different things. This is because when we see light our brain interprets the data our eyes receive and processes it to match our pre-programmed view of the world. In photography this isn't the case: the camera will record exactly what it sees unless you change something. Therefore, what you do with light and how you manage it will determine the message communicated by your images.

This section of the book will cover not only how light works but, more specifically, how light-sensitive photographic materials react to different lighting conditions, and what steps you can take, as the moulder and manipulator of light, to ensure your camera records light faithfully – whether that be faithful to the natural world or faithful to your personal vision.



Light is the essence of photography and learning how to use it is the key to mastering the photographic art.

# VISIBLE LIGHT

## What is meant by the term 'visible light'?

All light is formed by many different waves but only very few of them are visible to humans. These waves are what we term visible light and they form the light by which we see. There are other light waves invisible to the naked eye which, given the right set of circumstances (equipment, film type, conditions), are recorded by a camera. Some of these invisible rays have a positive effect on your photography (e.g. infrared) and some less so (e.g. ultraviolet).

The light spectrum

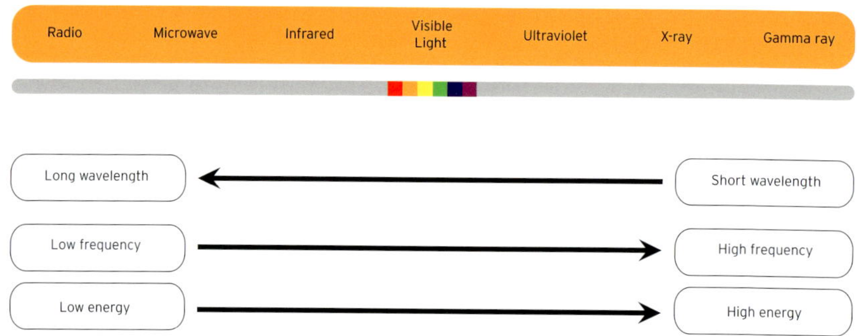


Light is formed of many different waves but the human eye can see only those in the visible light spectrum. Ultraviolet light can affect film and digital sensors, and infrared light can be used for creative photographic effects.

## How can I record infrared light?

Infrared light photography is possible using special films in conjunction with infrared filters. These films can be colour (e.g. Kodak Aerochrome III Infrared Film 1443) or black and white (e.g. Kodak's High-Speed Infrared HIE 135-36). You will need to use a manual camera to get the best results. Digital cameras can also be used for monochrome infrared photography by fixing an opaque filter (such as Hoya's R72) in front of the lens. An infrared effect can also be created from a standard digital image by using image-processing software, such as Adobe Photoshop.

**See also**

*Correction filters (page 44)*

### If ultraviolet (UV) light is invisible why do I need a UV filter?

Many users attach a UV filter to a lens simply as protection for the delicate (and expensive) front element. However, the main purpose of a UV filter is to block UV light, which, although invisible to humans, is recorded by photographic colour film (predominantly) and less so by digital sensors. UV light is most prevalent at high altitude and by the coast and causes an excessive blue colour cast. Using a UV filter will block UV light and reduce the likelihood of a blue cast occurring.

**See also**

*Correction filters (page 44)*

Ultraviolet light is more prevalent close to the coast and at high altitude. A UV filter will help to block UV rays from adversely affecting your images.

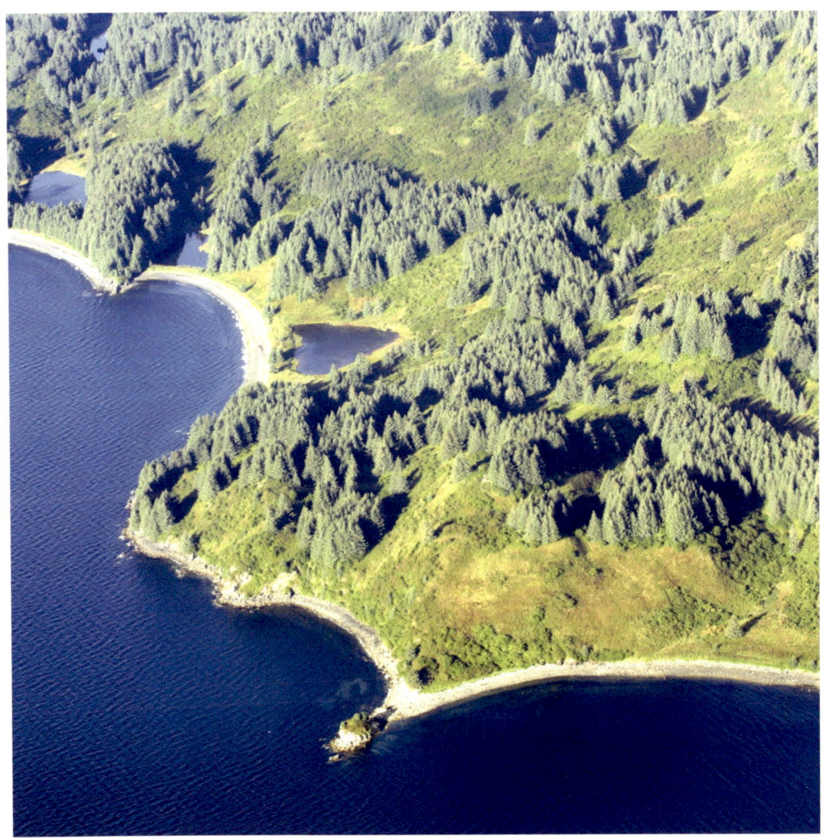

# THE COLOUR OF LIGHT

### What is meant by the term 'the colour of light'?

Visible light contains six principal colours - red, orange, yellow, green, blue and violet - most readily seen in rainbows. An equal mix of all colours produces colourless white light.

### What is the relevance in photography of the different colours of light?

The six colours of the visible spectrum, when mixed, are capable of producing the millions of colours that we see and recognise. When they are mixed all together in equal quantities they produce neutral white light.

#### Additive colours

Photographic devices such as cameras form colour by adding varying quantities of red, green and blue.

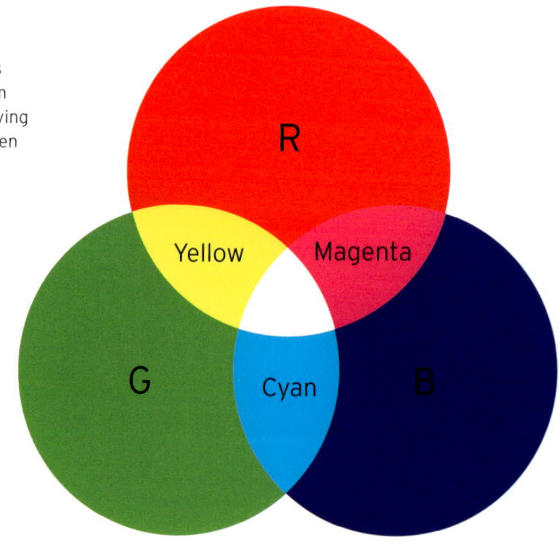


#### Subtractive colours

Printers form colour by subtraction using pigments to absorb certain wavelengths of white light. They use varying percentages of cyan, magenta and yellow.

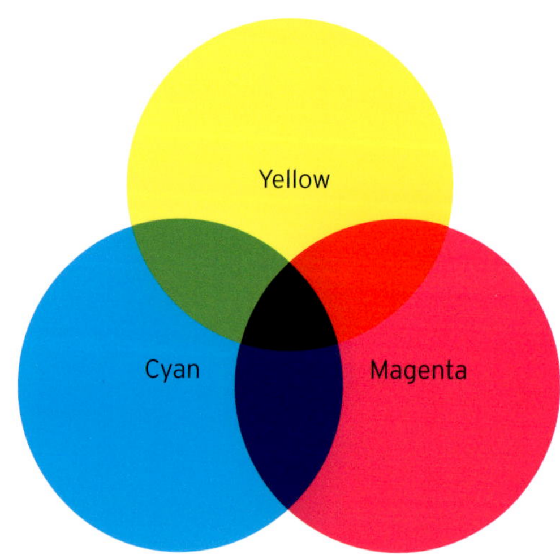

## What is meant by the term 'colour temperature'?

It's important to match colour temperature to the subject. This image of a frozen waterfall benefits from the cooler blue colour cast caused by the mid-day sun because we associate ice with cold.

Visible light is often referred to in terms of its colour temperature, which is affected by several factors including the type of lighting, the time of day and the weather. For example, sunlight on a clear day will be red-orange in the early morning, changing to yellow as it rises in the sky before turning white-blue at its peak, around noon. Humans do not detect differences in colour cast of different temperatures of light but photo-sensitive materials pick up these casts, which show in the final image.

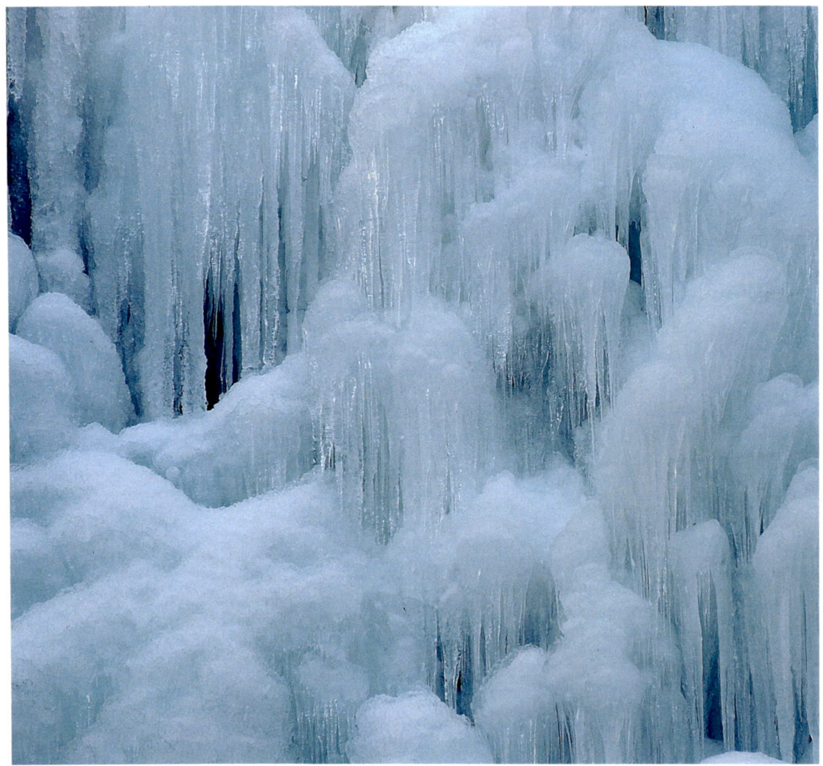

**See also**

*Natural light (page 50)*

Colour temperature of light

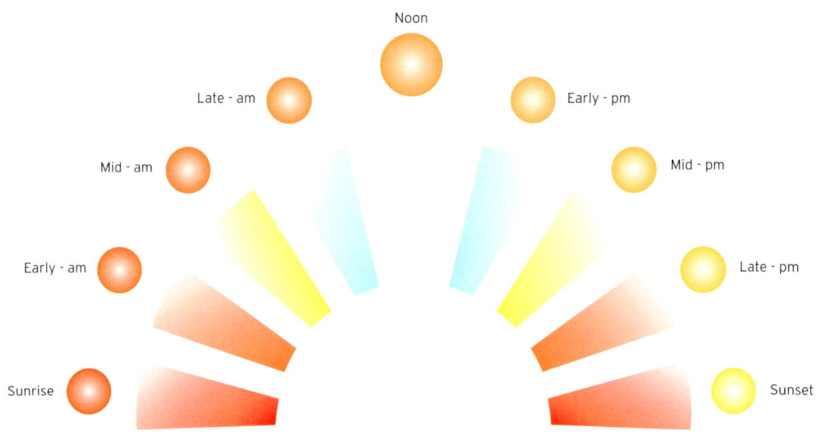


The colour temperature of light varies throughout the day, from warm reds and oranges in the early morning and late afternoon, through to cool blues around noon.

**Tip**

*A simple way to remember the colour cast created by sunlight throughout the day is to consider what happens to metal when it's heated. As you heat metal it first turns red (equivalent to sunrise), then orange (early morning), yellow (mid-morning) before finally turning blue-white hot (noon). The pattern is repeated in reverse as time moves towards evening.*

**See also**

*Artificial light (page 104)*

### Why do I need to be aware of colour temperature?

Light from different sources, or from the same source under different conditions, produces a colour cast, the extent of which depends on its colour temperature relative to how film or a digital sensor is balanced. For example, most photographic film is balanced to produce neutral white light under good weather daylight conditions. If you were to photograph a subject lit by a household light bulb (tungsten light) the resulting image would have an orange cast, because daylight and tungsten light have different colour temperatures. In order to record light accurately you need to know what effect different colour temperatures have on film and/or digital sensors in order to compensate as necessary to produce a neutral cast.

### How do I measure the colour temperature of light?

A colour temperature meter, which looks much like a standard hand-held light meter, can be used to accurately measure the colour temperature of light. Current models include the Minolta Color Meter IIIF, the Gossen Colormaster 3F and the Broncolor FCC. All digital cameras have a built-in meter for measuring colour temperature that is used in conjunction with the White Balance control to avoid unwanted colour casts.

**See also**

*The time of day (page 52)*
*Changing the colour temperature of natural light (page 62)*

The colour temperature of light changes depending on many factors. Understanding how light interacts with film or a photo sensor is important in visualising the effects of these changes in the final image.

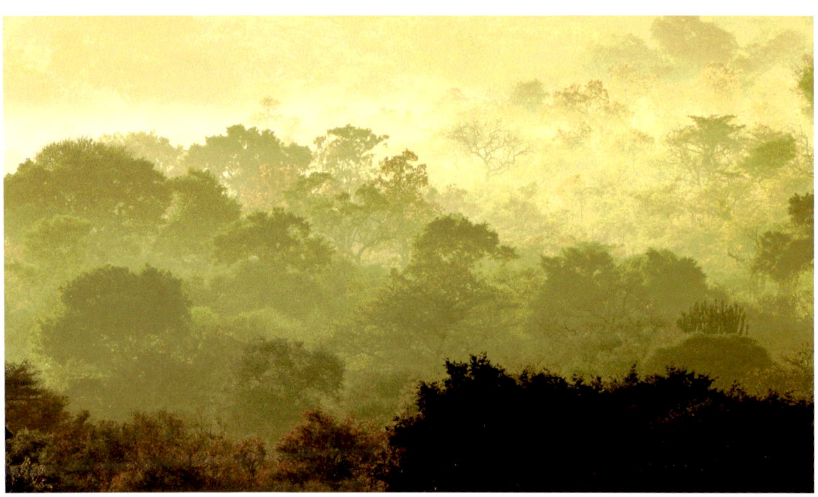

### How do I avoid colour casts when using film?

Film is available typically balanced for either daylight or tungsten light, and the first step is to ensure that you are using the film balanced closest to the lighting conditions you are photographing in. Typically, you would use daylight-balanced film when photographing outside or when using electronic flash. Tungsten-balanced film should be used when a tungsten light, such as a household light bulb, lights the subject. Even so, sometimes it's necessary to use optical correction filters to compensate for variances in colour temperature.

**See also**

*Correction filters (page 44)*

### How do I avoid colour casts when using a digital camera?

Digital cameras have a control called White Balance. This control enables the user to set a specific colour temperature to match the colour temperature of the light source. Theoretically, when the two are perfectly matched no colour cast will be apparent.

As well as the ability to set very specific Kelvin temperatures, most digital cameras have a number of pre-set WB settings for different conditions, such as sunlight, cloud, shade, tungsten and fluorescent lighting. There is also an Auto setting, which uses data from the built-in light temperature meter to assign a Kelvin value.

### Can I rely on the camera's Auto-WB function to gain accurate results?

This depends largely on what you consider an 'accurate result'. In the Auto-WB setting, the camera will always attempt to produce an image free from any colour cast. However, the camera can be influenced by external factors. For example, some cameras have an ambient sensor for measuring WB that sits on top of the prism finder. If a baseball cap is worn when photographing, the peak of the cap can shade the sensor and affect the result. You may not always want a neutral image lacking a colour cast. For example, sunrise and sunset images would lose their impact without the vibrant red/orange cast of the sun at this time.

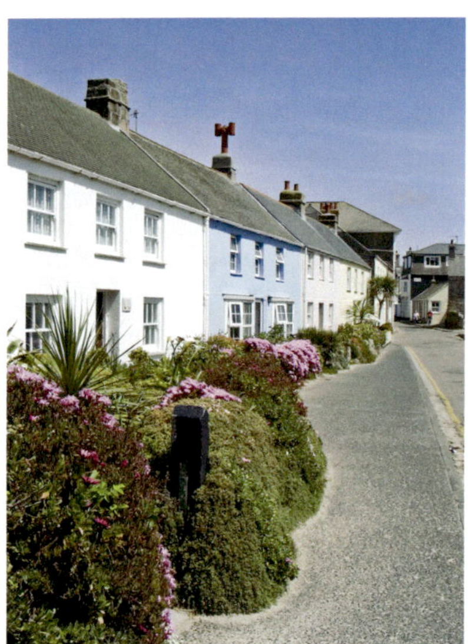

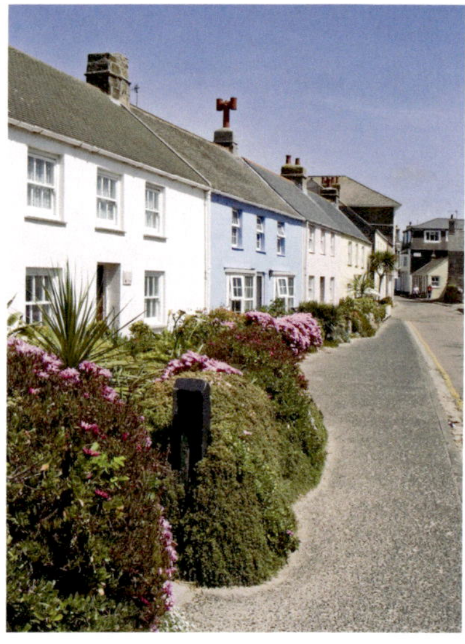

**See also**

*The time of day (page 52)*

The aim of the camera's Auto-WB setting is to produce a neutral result with no visible colour casts. However, a neutral image may not be appropriate. Here I have used Auto-WB for the first image, (left), and the pre-programmed Cloudy setting for the second image (right). The slight orange cast caused by the Cloudy setting has warmed the image for a more aesthetically pleasing result.

## What is reflected light?

Reflected light is what we use to make photographs. As the light falls on an object some of it is absorbed or travels straight through and some of it is reflected. It is this reflected light that allows us to see (and photograph) objects.

## What are the characteristics of reflected light?

When light falls on an object, how it responds is governed by science. Omitting the really technical bit (it has much to do with photons, electrons and atoms), it may travel straight through the object (transparency), be absorbed, reflected (singly or in multiples), scattered or refracted. Of course, what happens to the light affects the possibilities for photographing it. For example, the more transparent an object the easier it is to photograph through without degrading the quality of the light entering the lens. The rainbow colours in soap bubbles and patterns made by oil spills on wet roads, both of which make interesting photographic subjects, are caused by multiple-surface reflectance.

**See also**

*Polarising filters (page 45)*

Characteristics of light

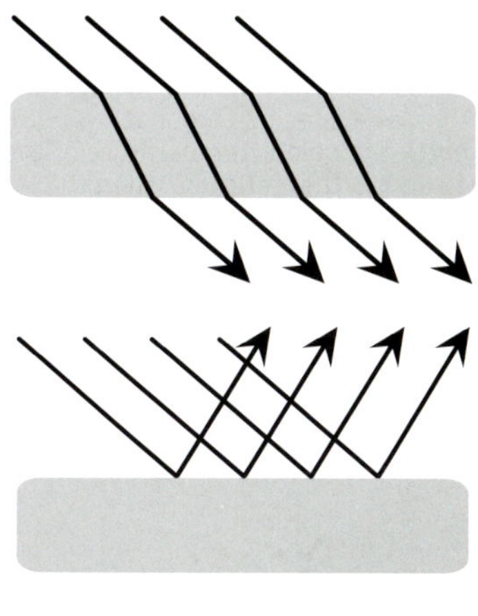

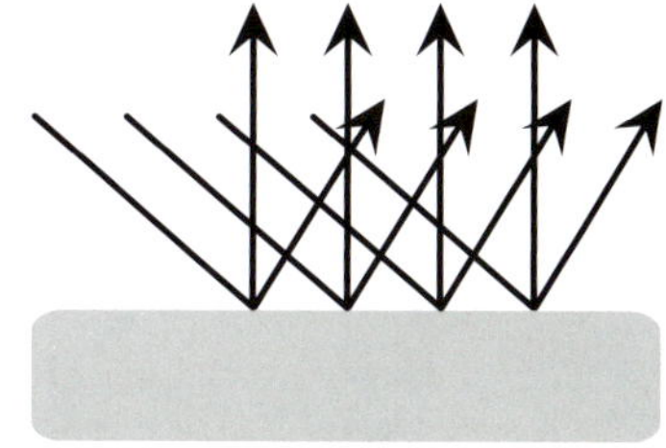

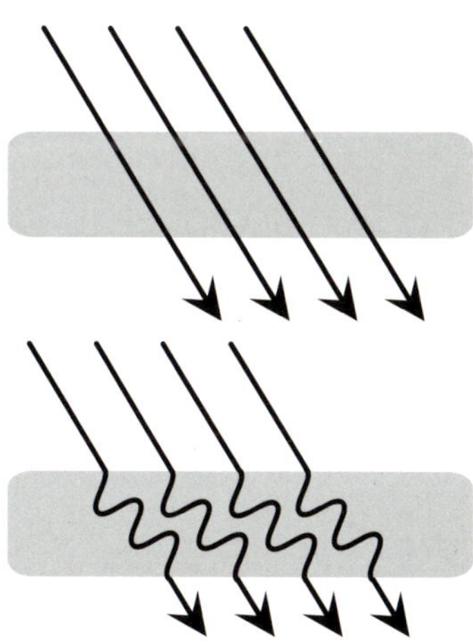

When light falls on an object it reacts in different ways depending on the properties of the subject.

# INTENSITY OF LIGHT

## What affects the intensity of light?

The intensity (strength) of light depends on the distance between the light source and the subject, and the size of the light source. The closer the light source is to the subject the greater the level of illumination. Similarly, a direct (small) light source produces harder, more intense light than a larger light source, which typically produces softer, less intense lighting. Think about this in terms of macro photography. A flash unit placed within a few inches of the subject is liable to produce too strong (intense) illumination. By using a diffused flash unit, or by moving the flash unit further from the subject, the intensity of light is reduced.

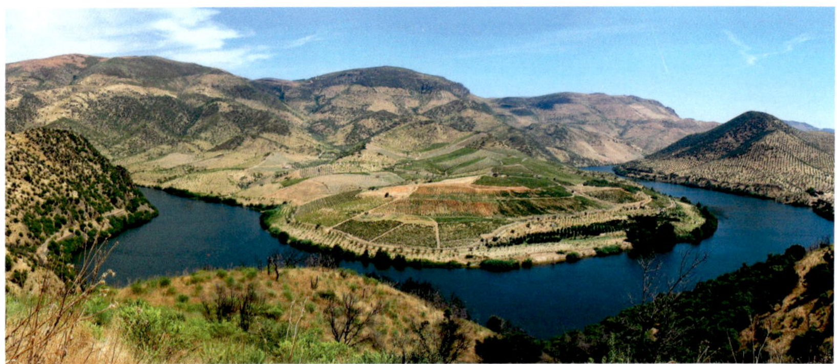

Outdoors, the intensity of light is affected by the weather. Direct sunlight is intense (above) while cloud cover reduces the intensity of light (facing opposite).

## Can I control the intensity of light?

With artificial lighting you typically have complete control over the intensity of the light. For example, you can reduce the power of the flash to emit less light, move the flash closer to or further away from the subject and you can alter the size of the light source by using various flash attachments.

Natural light is harder to control but not impossible. Light source to subject distance is, to all intents and purposes, fixed but you can alter the size of the light source by using natural diffusers, such as clouds, or artificial diffusers, which will convert a small source of light (direct sunlight) to a large source of light (omni-directional, or scattered, sunlight).

### See also

*Flash accessories (page 112)*
*Panel reflectors and diffusers (page 49)*

### Tip

*It is useful to note that the Inverse Square Law only really applies to flash photography, as the distance of the sun from the subject remains largely unchanged, at least in terms of photography.*

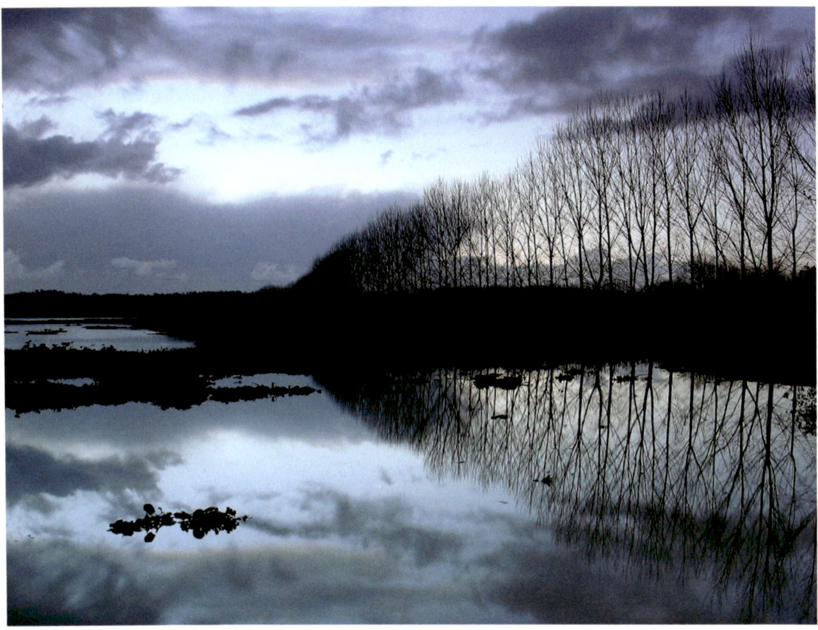

## What is the Inverse Square Law?

The Inverse Square Law is a mathematical equation used to measure the effect of changing the light-to-subject distance. When halving the distance between the light and the subject, the level of illumination quadruples. Conversely, doubling the distance between the light and the subject reduces to a quarter the intensity of light.

This equation is useful when photographing in a studio environment, as it is possible to reassess exposures accurately after making changes to the position of any lighting in relation to the subject. For example, if you reduce the level of illumination by a quarter then you must compensate by increasing the exposure by four times.

The Inverse Square Law

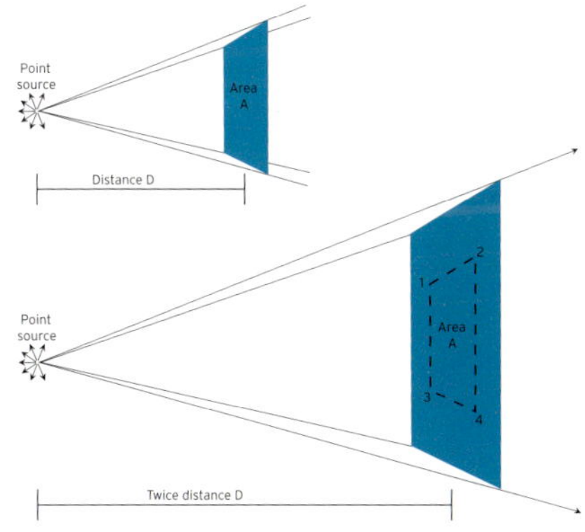


The Inverse Square Law relates to the effect on light intensity caused by moving the light source closer or further from the subject.

# QUALITY OF LIGHT

### What is meant by the term 'quality of light'?

Quality of light refers to how hard or soft the light is. For example, light from an unobstructed point source, such as the sun on a clear day or a flash unit, is referred to as hard lighting, as it produces a greater degree of contrast and well-defined, hard-edged shadows. When light is diffused, for example sunlight filtered through cloud cover or a flash unit fitted with a soft box, then the quality of light softens, producing less contrast in the scene and less well-defined shadows with softer edges.

Light is considered either hard or soft in quality. Hard lighting, from a direct point source, creates well-defined shadows (below). Soft lighting, from a diffused source, softens the edges of shadows and makes them less pronounced (facing opposite).

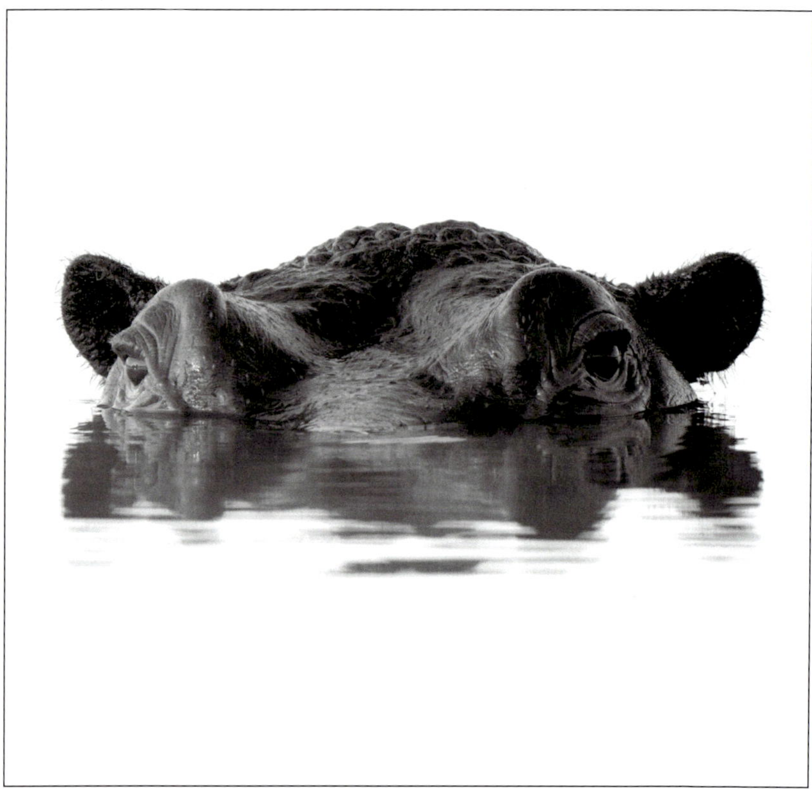

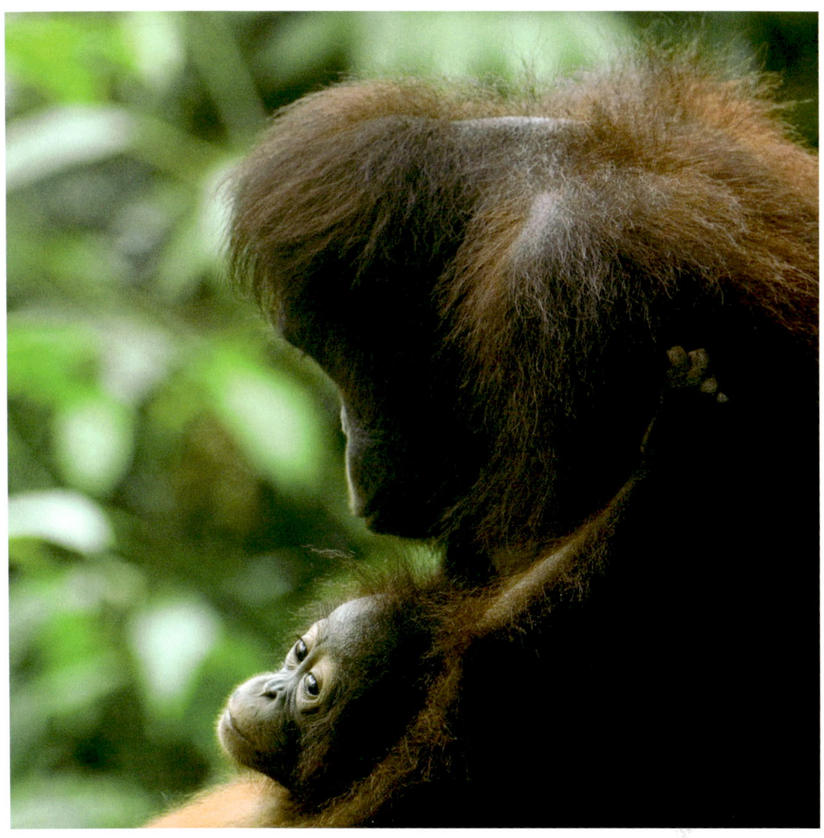

**What affects the quality of light?**

The level of diffusion (or scattering) affects the quality of light. A heavy layer of clouds, for example, will greatly soften the hard quality of direct sunlight, reducing contrast and minimising shadows. This can be seen easily if you stand outside on a sunny day and compare your shadow with that created on a cloudy day. There are also various accessories that can be used with flash to soften the quality of the light emitted by the flash.

**See also**

*Flash accessories (page 112)*

### Can I control the quality of light?

In much the same way that you can control the intensity of light, you can also control the quality of light. Again, this is more easily achieved in a studio environment where you have complete control over lighting, and where the use of reflectors and diffusers can alter the quality of light from very hard to very soft.

Outside, you have limited control of the quality of lighting. The obvious means of controlling the quality of light is by choosing the type of weather conditions in which to shoot. Choose to go out on a cloudy day and you are choosing a soft quality of light in which to photograph. It is also possible in some situations, such as when shooting outdoors, even for portraiture, to use diffusers to soften the quality of hard, direct light from the sun.

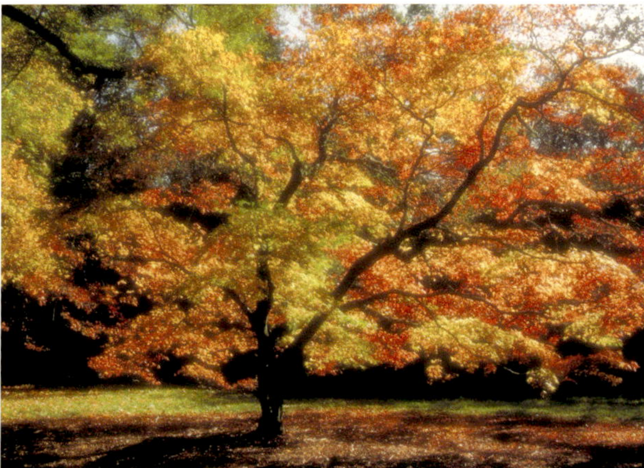

**See also**

*Panel reflectors and diffusers (page 49)*

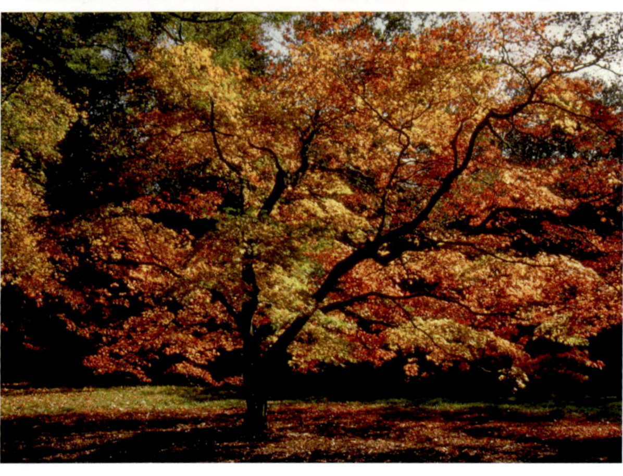

Diffusers provide the opportunity to add a misty, dreamlike appearance to shots. The first image (top) was taken using a standard diffuser filter, whilst the second image (bottom) was taken without a diffuser. The diffuser has not blurred the image; it is still critically sharp but has the soft, diffused image overlaid.

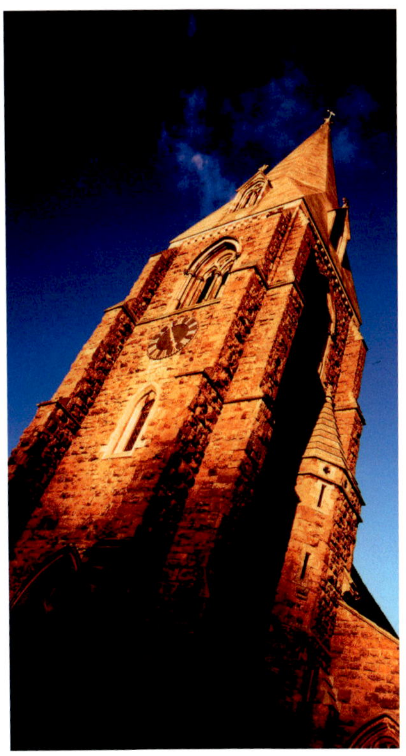

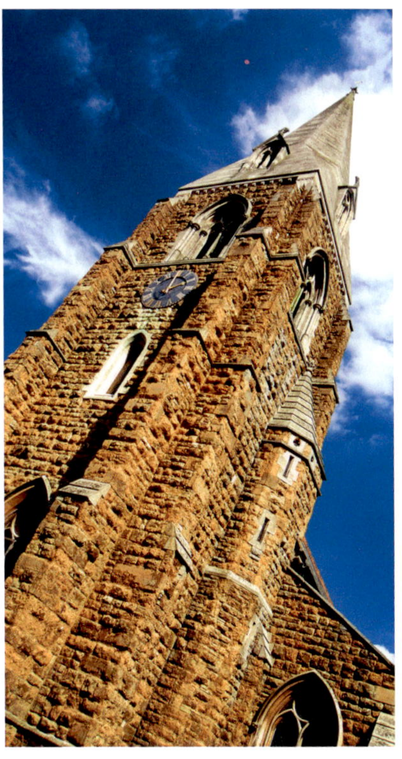

Contrast helps to create form, a sense of three dimensions. Without contrast images can look flat and lack depth.

### How does the quality of light affect contrast?

Contrast is the variance between areas of light and dark. When the quality of light is hard and shadows are more intense and well-defined, contrast is greater. When the quality of light is soft, shadows are softer with less well-defined edges, resulting in a lower level of contrast. Therefore, contrast is greatest in hard (point) lighting and less prevalent when lighting is from a diffused, or omni-directional, source, such as sunlight on an overcast day.

# DIRECTION OF LIGHT

## Is there a 'best' direction of light in photography?

The answer is yes...and no. The direction from which light falls on a subject will determine where and if shadows appear, and it is shadows that help to give a subject its visual form. For many subjects, lighting from the side is often considered ideal, as side lighting will cause shadows to form on the unlit side of the subject. When used in portraiture, for example, this helps us to see that a face or body has contours and is not two-dimensional. Similarly, in landscape photography shadows created by side lighting help to create a sense of depth, as well as form. However, side lighting is less suitable for revealing detail in, for example, a building; in this case front lighting is more suitable.

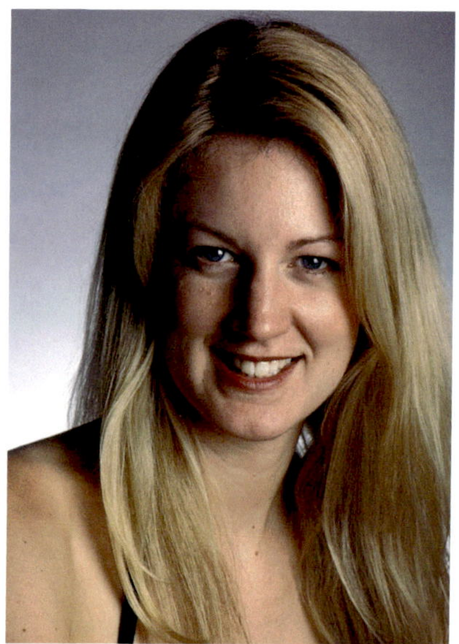

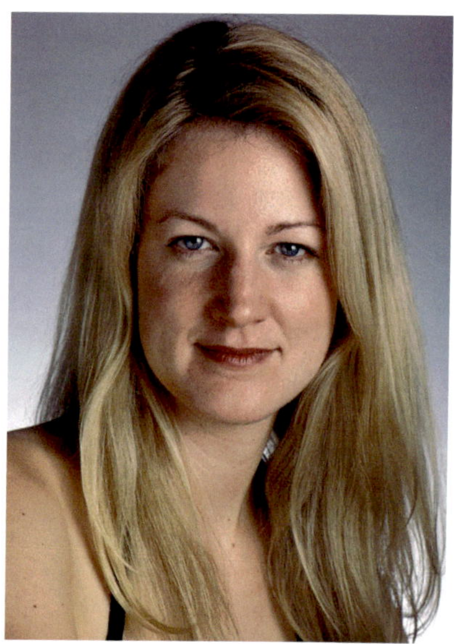

The direction from which a subject is lit will determine where shadows fall, which will change the aesthetics of the image.

### Tip

*A simple way to explore how different qualities and directions of light affect how a subject appears is to run a simple test. You'll need a suitable subject (a vase will do), an angle-poise lamp and a thin white cloth. Place the vase on a table, set up your camera and use the lamp to light the vase from several different directions (side, front, back, above), taking a picture for each lighting position. To experiment with the quality of light, run the same test but with the thin white cloth covering the front of the light shade. This will turn the hard quality of the lamp to a softer, omni-directional light.*

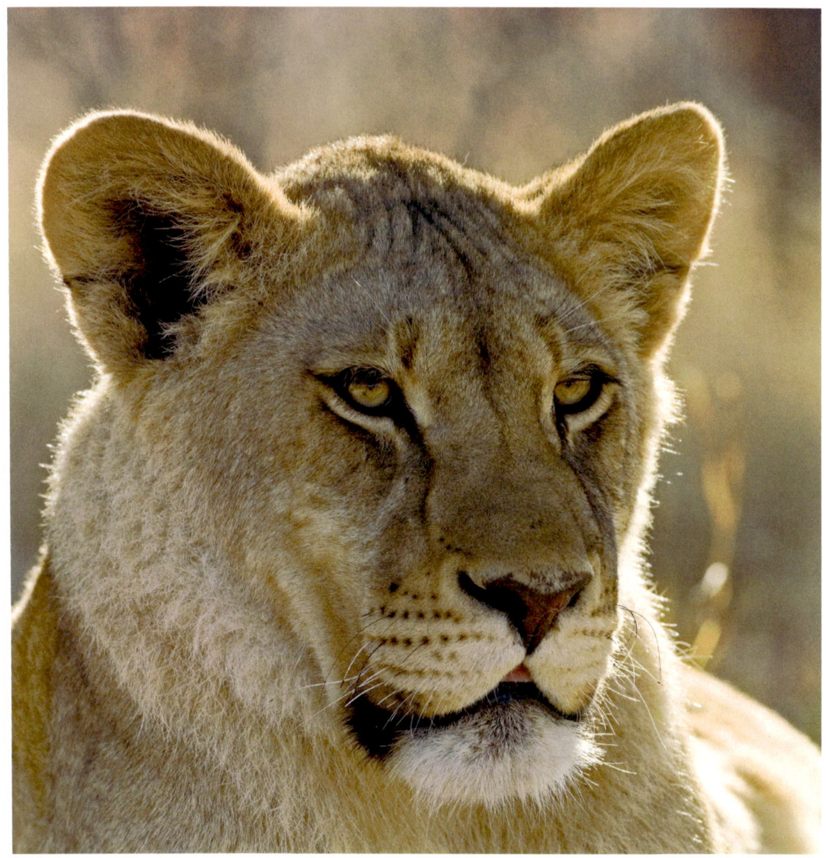

Exposing for the shadow area has produced rim lighting around the head of this backlit lioness.

## When would I use backlighting?

Backlighting will produce silhouettes or rim lighting, depending on the exposure used (exposing for the highlights produces a silhouette, exposing for the shadows produces rim lighting). Backlighting is ideal for creating atmospheric images of subjects such as people, animals and landscapes.

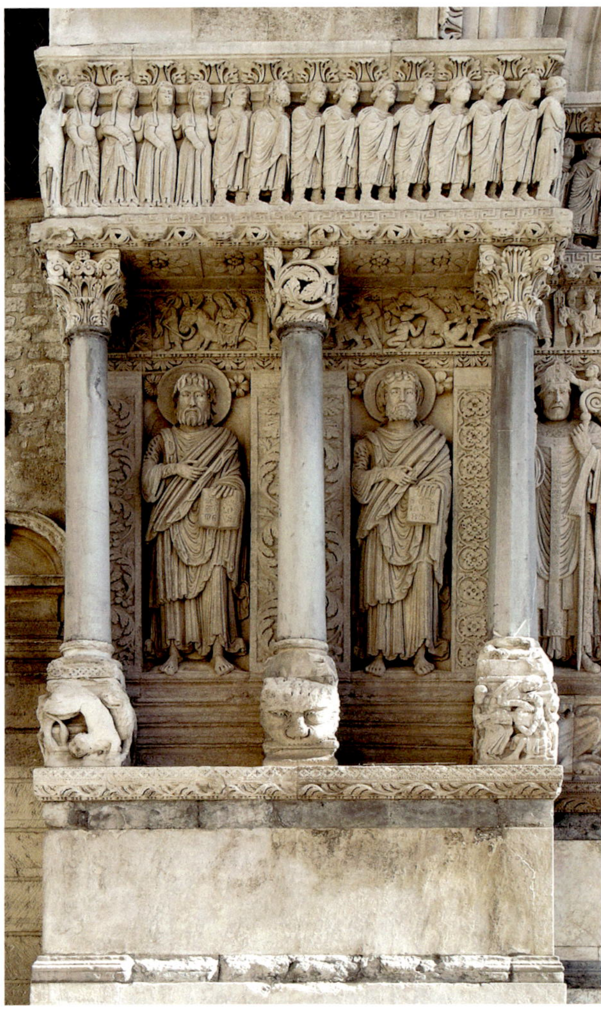

Front lighting is ideal for revealing detail in subjects such as buildings.

### When would I use front lighting?

Many books advise against photographing with the light directly in front of the subject and often this is good advice. For example, people and animals rarely look their best when lit by light coming from head on. However, front lighting is ideal for revealing detail and is often used when photographing objects such as buildings for record purposes.

### When would I use side lighting?

Side lighting is often considered the best direction for lighting and should be used when you want to reveal form and depth. Portrait photographers will typically light their subjects from the side and landscape photographers find side lighting best for creating images with a three-dimensional appearance.

**See also**

*Suggested studio light set-ups (page 139)*

Side lighting is ideal for revealing form and creating a sense of depth and three dimensions.

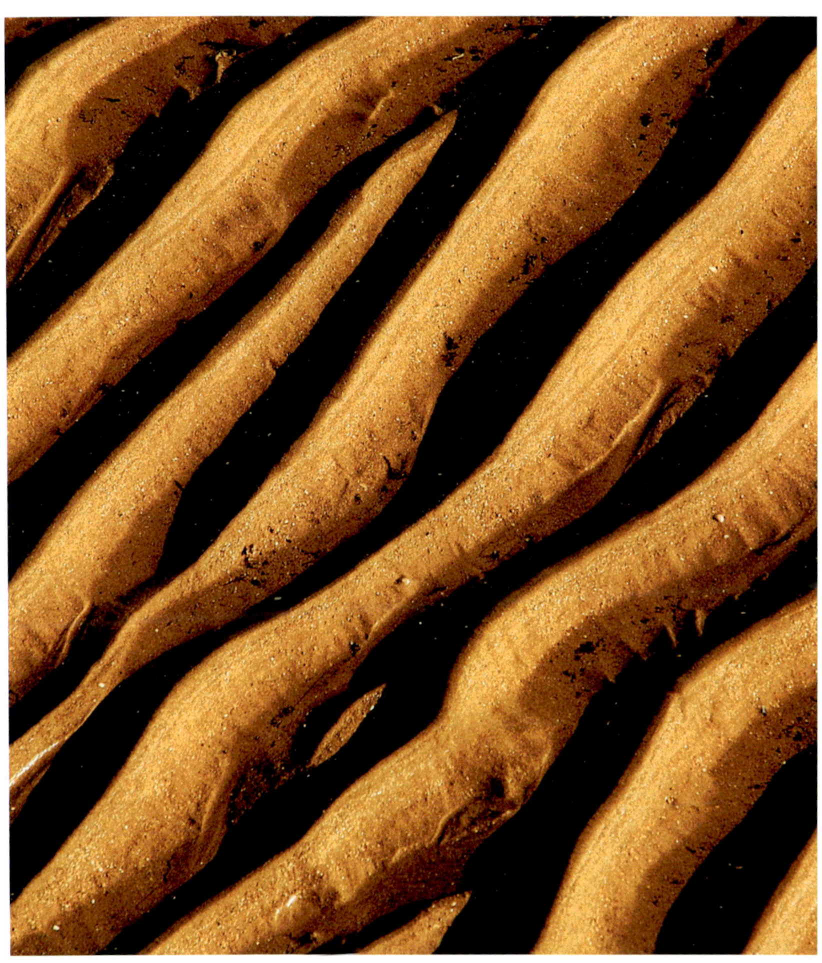

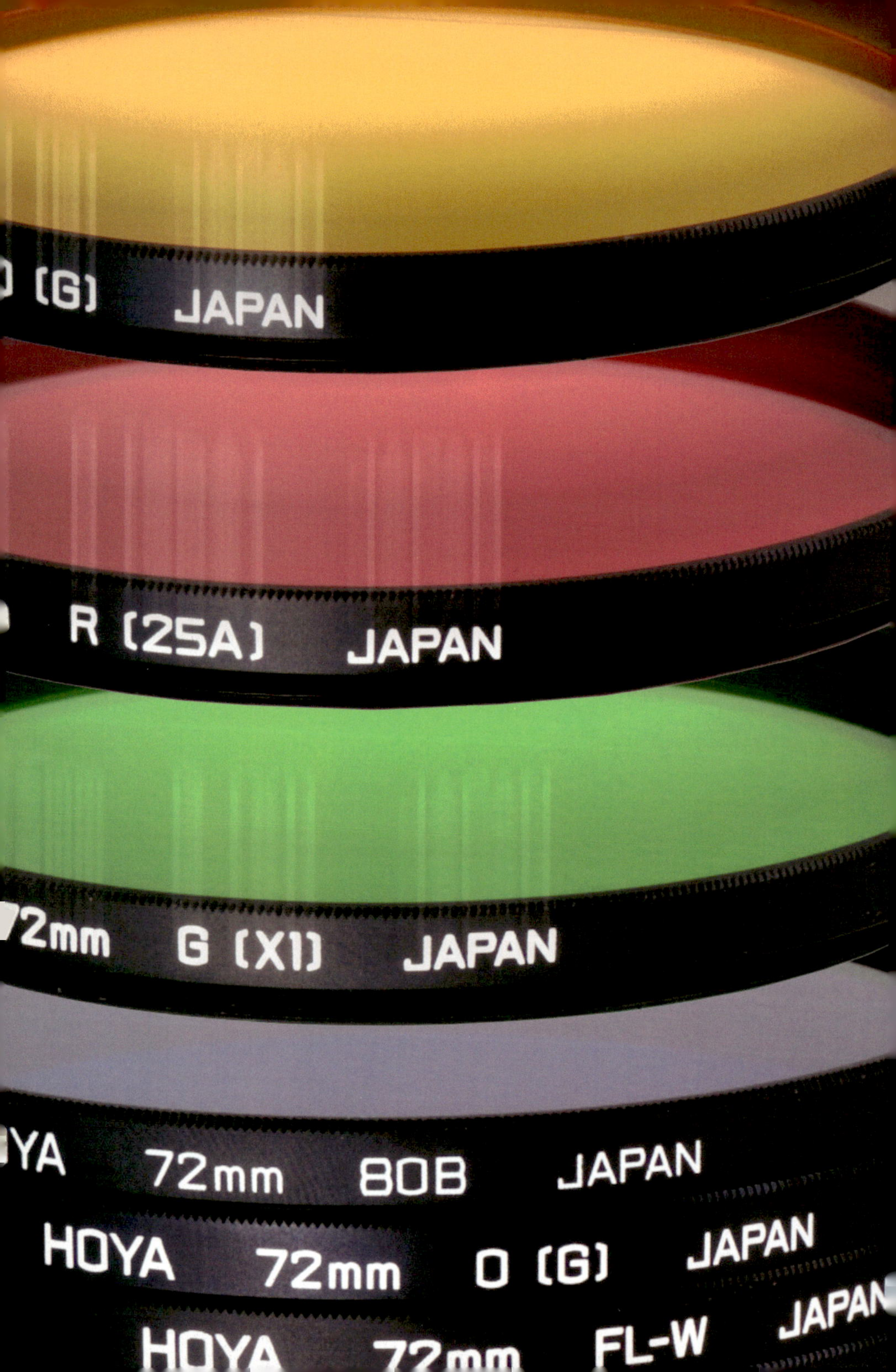

O (G) JAPAN
R (25A) JAPAN
72mm G (X1) JAPAN
YA 72mm 80B JAPAN
HOYA 72mm O (G) JAPAN
HOYA 72mm FL-W JAPAN

SECTION TWO

# EQUIPMENT AND CAMERA FUNCTIONS

Sometimes the ability to manage, manipulate and exploit light is dependent on the correct bit of equipment being available. I'm not talking here about cameras and lenses specifically, more about the add-ons that can make the difference between achieving the shot you want or ending up with something inferior, which is simply all the camera is capable of recording unaided.

Equipment for lighting falls into two categories: camera-related functions and accessories, and flash-related accessories. Accessories for flash are covered later on (see Flash accessories, page 112). In this section of the book I am dealing only with equipment that relates to the camera, such as light meters, filters of varying types and varieties, reflectors and diffusers, and flash units.

Often the different pieces of equipment discussed here are overlooked, perhaps because the reason for their use and the practicality of using them is not always explained as clearly as it should be, if at all. Here I hope to change that. I appreciate that lens hoods, for example, aren't sexy in the way a new DSLR is considered to be. However, knowing when and how to use one or, to take another example, understanding why it may be necessary to carry with you 20 or so different filters, are the details that set professionals apart. They are the real difference between another 'if only...' shot and the ability to make consistently compelling images.



What the camera sees and what you see aren't always the same thing. We use the tools at our disposal to manipulate light for a more faithful reproduction.

# LIGHT METERS AND EXPOSURE

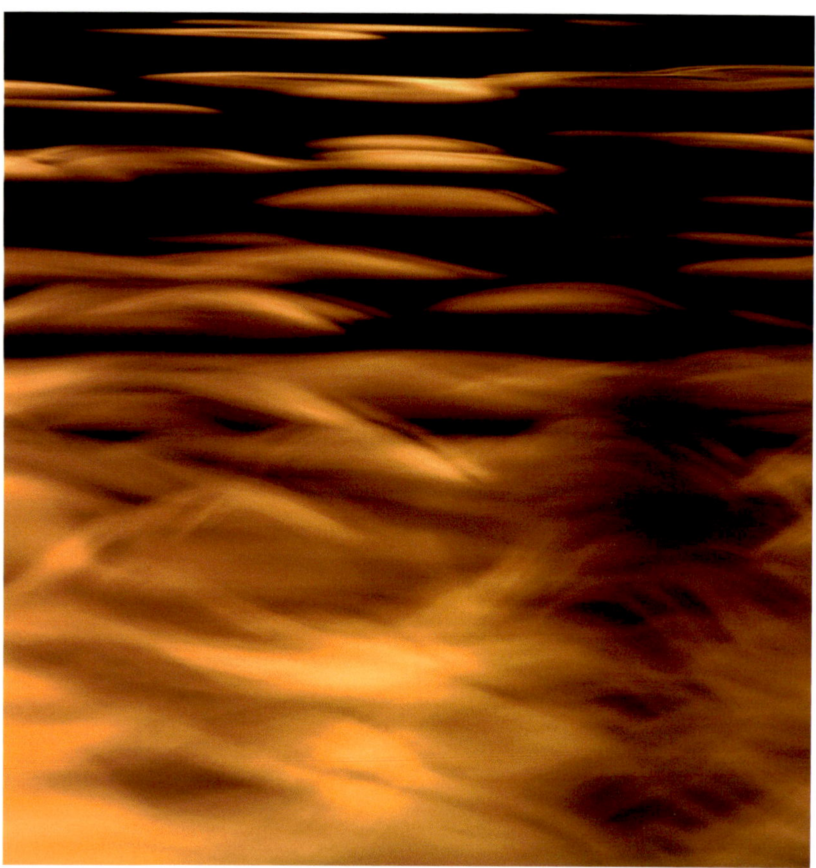

Understanding how camera functions and equipment can help change the visual impression of an image will help you to create images that stand out from the crowd. Here I used a combination of optical filters and a hand-held light meter to create an abstract image of water on a pond.

## What is a light meter?

Light meters measure the intensity of light. In relation to photography they produce an exposure value (EV), which is used (either manually or automatically) to determine an exposure setting given in terms of a lens aperture/shutter speed combination.

Photographic light meters are typically built into the camera, and are referred to as through-the-lens (TTL) meters because they measure the intensity of light entering through the camera lens. Hand-held spot and incident light meters are also available and will be discussed later in this chapter (see page 41).

Dynamic range and film latitude

Film and digital sensors have a limited ability to record detail across a broad range of brightness, restricting their ability to retain detail in areas of highlight and shadow simultaneously.

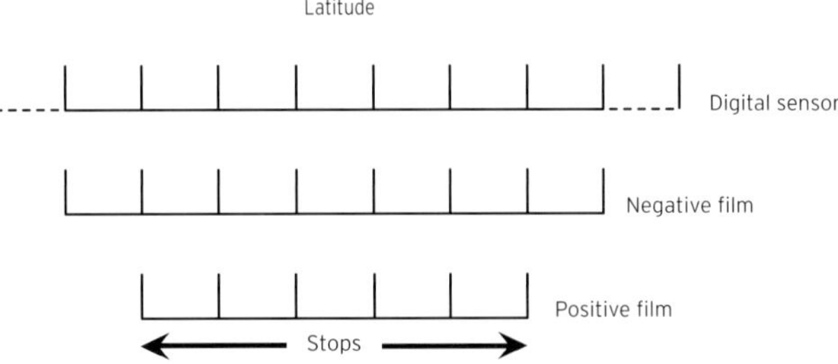


## How does my camera calculate exposure?

If your camera has a light meter it is probably a through-the-lens (TTL) meter. A TTL light meter measures the intensity of reflected light entering the lens. As such, TTLs take into account any light-absorbing accessories that may be positioned in front of the lens or between lens and camera, such as filters or close-up extenders.

Now, it is very important to understand that reflected light meters are calibrated to see everything in the world as 18% grey and will provide an exposure calculation based on your subject being 18% grey, whether it is or it isn't. For example, if you've ever wondered why snow, when photographed using the camera's auto-exposure function, typically appears grey in the final image it's because your camera's light meter thinks that snow is grey - 18% grey to be exact.

The reason for this 18% grey - or medium (middle) tone - calibration is that no reflected light meter can distinguish between different tones (shades of grey) and so the manufacturers have to set a line in the sand. That line has been determined as 18% grey, being exactly halfway between film's ability to record detail in shadows and highlights.

What this means is that when you (or your camera) take a light reading you must ask yourself the question: 'is the subject I'm photographing medium-tone (18%) grey, or is it lighter than or darker than medium-tone?' If the subject is medium-tone then the camera will produce a technically accurate exposure. However, if the subject is lighter than or darker than medium-tone, then the camera is liable to under-expose (lighter subjects) or over-expose (darker subjects) because it is always trying to achieve a medium-tone, 18% grey result.

Once you know that the camera will always provide exposure calculations based on the subject being medium-toned, exposure becomes much simpler. Now you just have to consider how much to compensate for subjects that are lighter or darker than medium-tone.

## What are the different metering modes on my camera?

Typically the TTL light meter in the camera can be set to measure light from different areas of the scene using the metering mode selector. Most cameras have three metering mode options: multi-segment metering, centre-weighted (or average) metering and spot metering modes.

**Multi-segment metering**
Different camera manufacturers refer to their version of multi-segment metering using different names. For example, Nikon calls it matrix metering, Canon calls it evaluative metering and Sony/Minolta calls it honeycomb pattern metering. However, to all intents and purposes, the systems work the same way, by measuring the level of brightness in different sections of the viewfinder screen to assess the brightness range and calculate an appropriate exposure value.

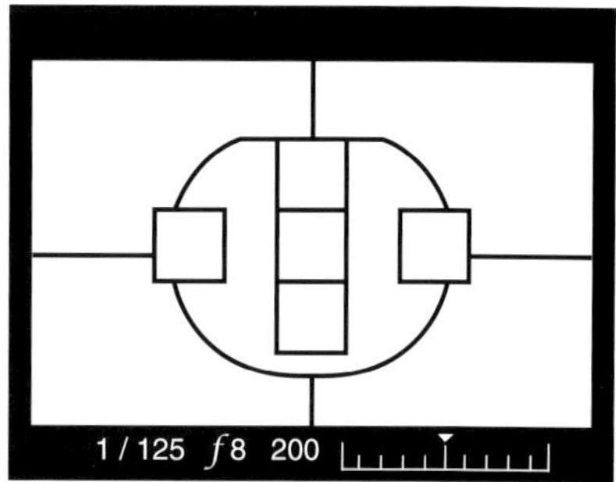


**Centre-weighted metering**
When you look through the viewfinder of your camera you'll probably see a circle etched in the centre of the screen. In centre-weighted metering mode, the majority of light information used to calculate an exposure value (about 75%) is taken from this centre portion. The remainder is taken from the area around the centre circle.

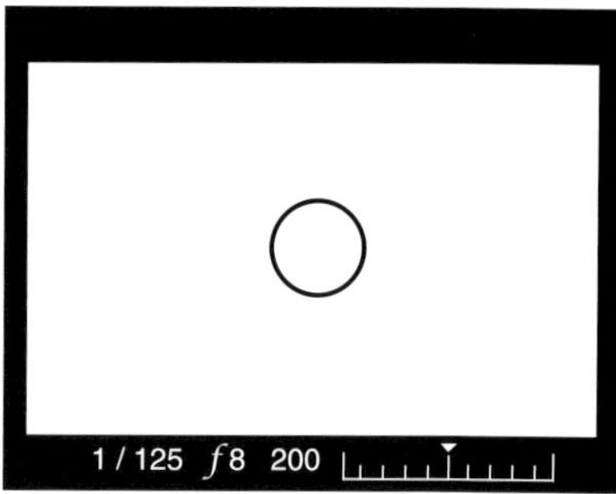


**Spot metering**
When set to spot metering mode the meter measures the intensity of light from a tiny area of the scene, usually around 3-5%.

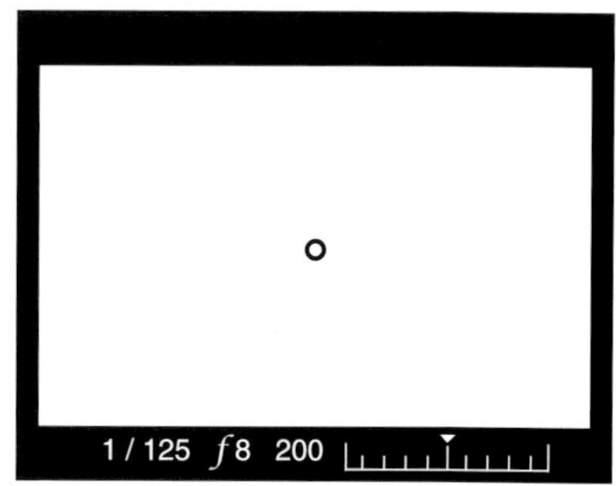

## When would I use multi-segment metering mode?

Multi-segment metering is ideal for occasions when you want to spend little time worrying about exposure and are happy to allow the camera to make an assessment of the lighting conditions. To be fair most manufacturers' multi-segment metering systems are highly accurate, even in quite complex lighting conditions. The downside is that they still make an assessment based on what the camera sees and not on what you see or are trying to create.

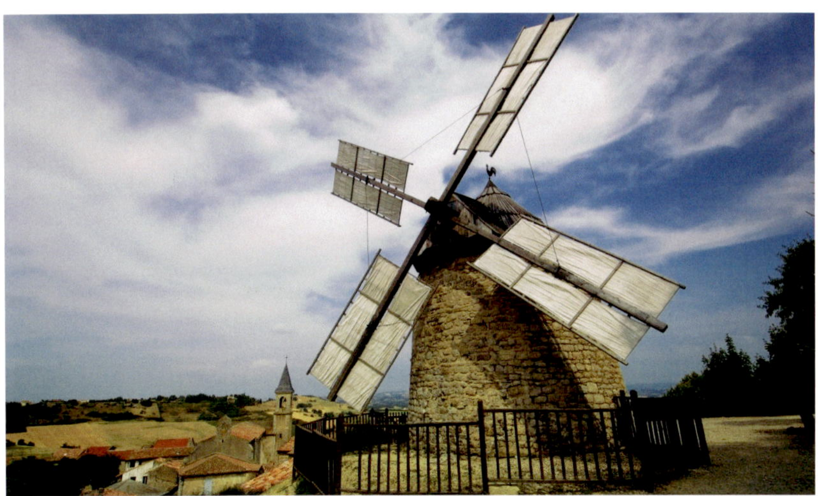

Even in complex lighting conditions the sophisticated multi-segment metering systems in modern cameras are able to produce acceptable results.

## When would I use centre-weighted metering mode?

Centre-weighted metering is often considered ideal for portraiture, where the subject fills the centre of the frame and the (less important) background plays a less significant role in the composition.

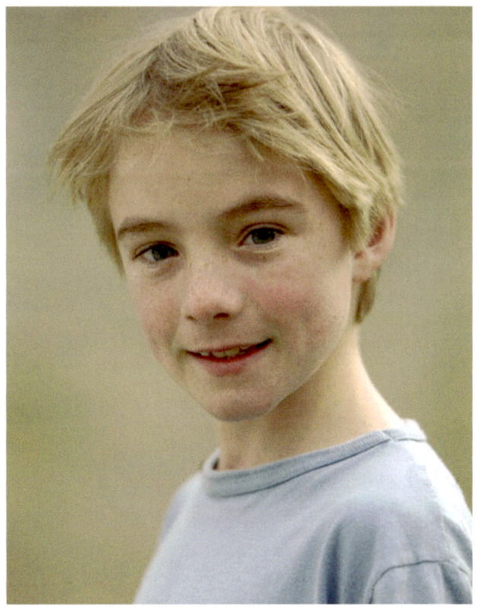

Centre-weighted through the lens metering is ideal for portraiture.

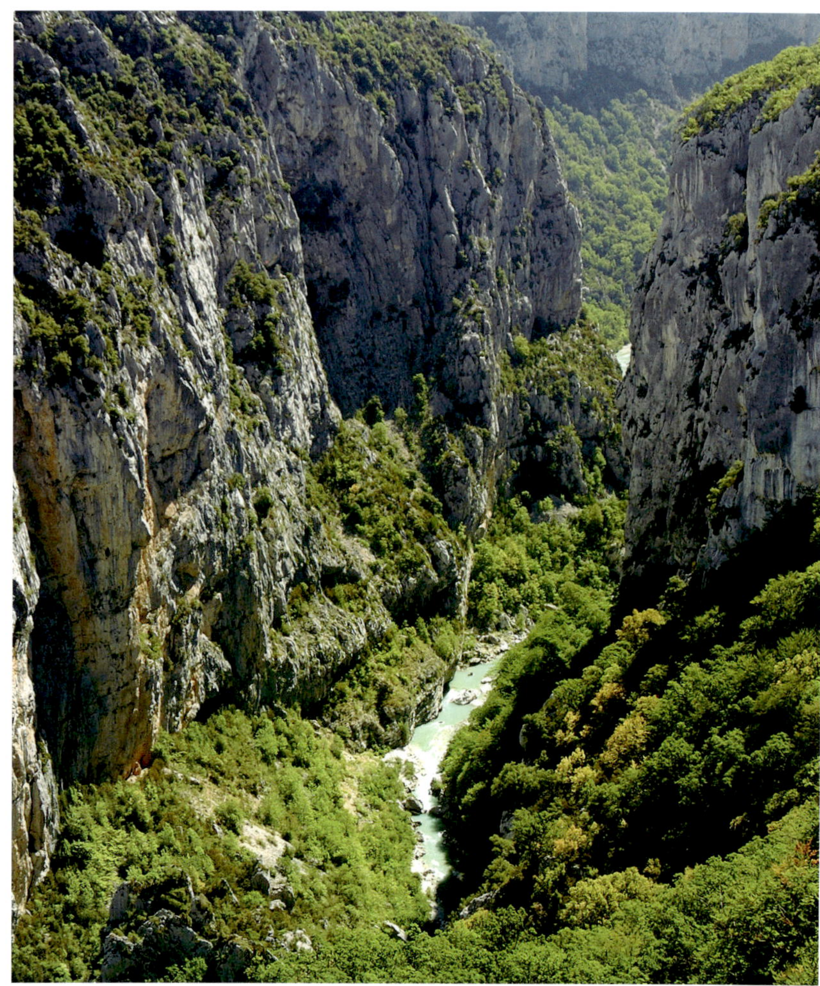

Spot metering allows the photographer to take complete control of the exposure process to produce ideal results, even when lighting conditions are complex.

**When would I use spot metering mode?**

Spot metering is used when you want to have a greater degree of control over calculating an exposure value for a scene where the lighting is complex, or where you are attempting to produce a more artistic image. You would also use spot metering when calculating the subject brightness range, i.e. the difference in stops between the lightest and darkest areas of the scene, a typical application here being landscape photography.

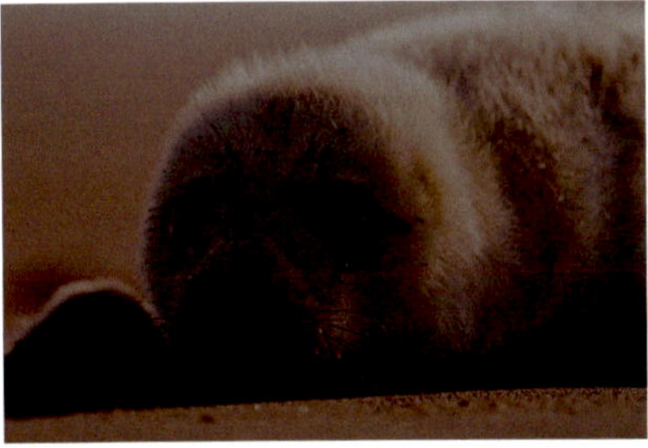

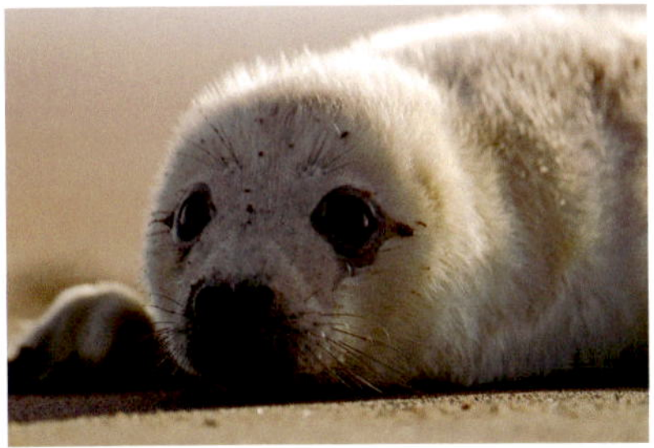

The backlighting on the seal pup has caused the camera's auto-exposure system to under-expose the animal's face. By applying +1 stop exposure compensation (over-exposing the camera's auto reading) I have brightened the image for a more faithful result.

### What is the purpose of exposure compensation?

Using the camera's auto exposure compensation function, the calculated exposure value (EV) determined by the in-built TTL meter reading is adjusted by the level of exposure compensation applied. For example, if the camera assesses the EV as 8 and you have applied a 1-stop increase in exposure via the exposure compensation function, then the camera will automatically set an exposure for EV 7 (1 stop open from EV 8). The opposite would apply when reducing exposure.

Therefore, exposure compensation can be used to apply the necessary exposure adjustments for subjects that are lighter or darker than medium-tone. For example, if you were to photograph snow, the camera would give a meter reading that assumes the snow is medium (18%) grey. As snow is around 2 stops brighter than medium tone, by applying +2 stops exposure compensation, the camera will add 2 stops extra brightness to the scene, ensuring that the snow appears in print as white.

### How do I recognise a medium-tone subject?

The ability to recognise tonality comes from experience. However, you can speed the process by carrying a Kodak grey card and comparing the relative tonality of your subject with that of the card. For example, consider the brightness of a daffodil compared to medium-grey. When placed next to each other the flower is obviously brighter than the card. This is the simplest and quickest way to learn to see and interpret tone. In the meantime, some useful guides for medium-toned everyday subjects are: lawn-green grass, clear blue sky around noon and poppy red.

**See also**

*Understanding light (page 12)*
*Natural light (page 50)*

### How much exposure compensation should I apply for non-middle tone subjects?

Again the ability to assess the difference in stops between tones comes from experience. Here's a quick guide to help you.

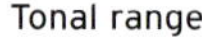
Tonal range

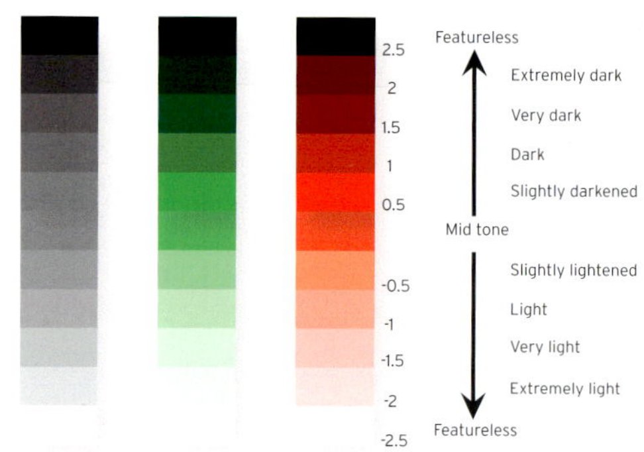


This diagram is a guide to the difference levels of brightness, measured in stops, across the tonal range.

### What is exposure bracketing?

Bracketing is the process of taking two or more near-identical images at exposure values above and below the metered value. For example, say your camera calculates an EV of 8. You might take one picture of the scene with exposure settings equivalent to EV 8, another at exposure settings equivalent to EV 7 and another with exposure settings equivalent to EV 9. This would give you three exposures, one exposed as the camera metered the scene, one over-exposed by 1 stop from the camera's calculated EV and one under-exposed by 1 stop from the camera's calculated EV. The purpose of bracketing is to ensure an accurate exposure is obtained, even in difficult lighting conditions.

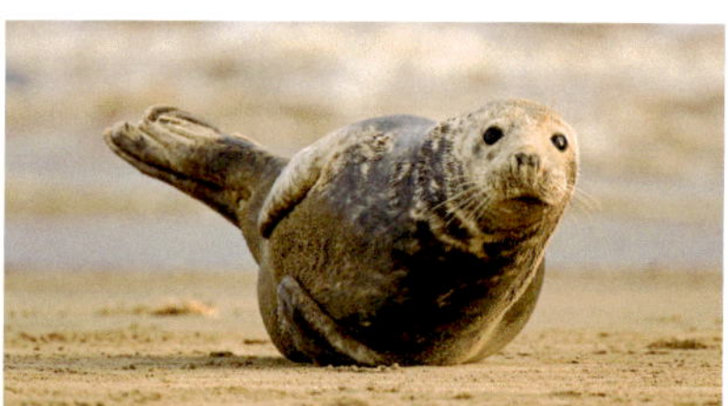

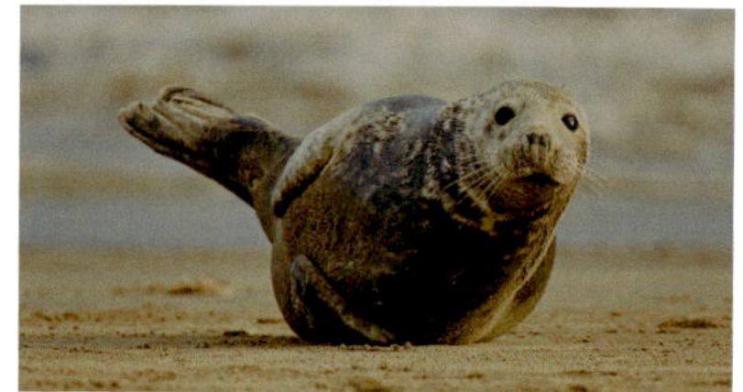

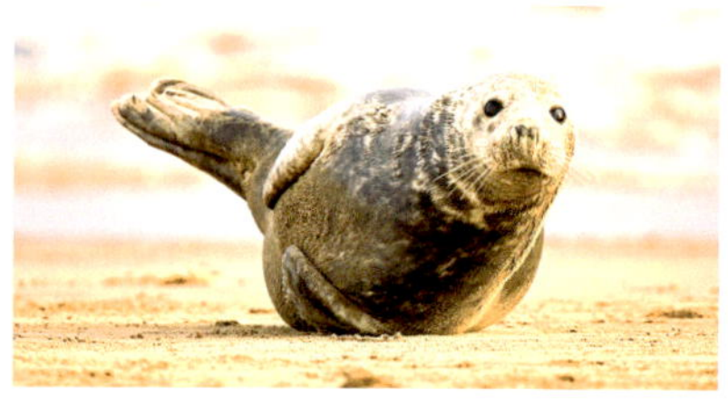

A set of three bracketed images. The first image (top) was taken at the camera's auto-exposure reading plus 1 stop, the second image (middle) at the camera's auto-exposure reading with no adjustment, and the final image (bottom) at the camera's auto-exposure reading minus 1 stop.

## How does a hand-held meter work?

Hand-held meters were common before in-built light meters became standard in cameras. There are two main types of photographic light meter (excluding a flash light meter), which are the reflected-light spot meter and the incident light meter.

A reflected-light spot meter operates in much the same way as a built-in meter except that it doesn't measure the light actually entering the lens and therefore takes no account of any accessories attached to the lens. On the positive side, hand-held spot meters typically measure the light from a tighter area of the scene, around 1 degree. This makes them more accurate when measuring specific areas of light.

An incident light meter works very differently in that it reads the light falling on a subject, as opposed to the light reflecting off the subject. This has the advantage that the reflectance and absorption properties of the subject need not be taken into account but the disadvantage that ideally the light meter should be close to the subject when the reading is taken.

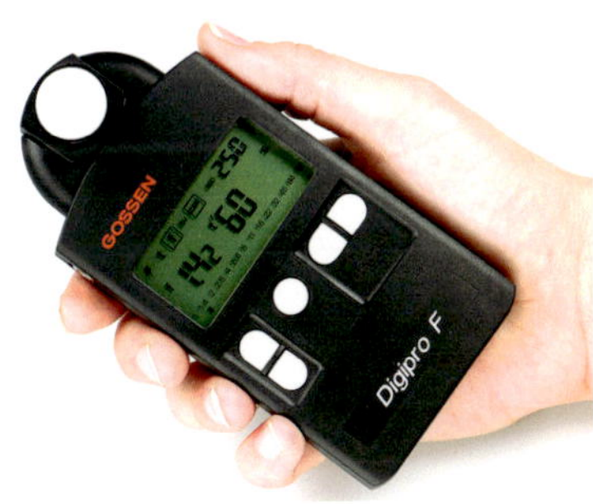


An incident light meter can be used outdoors or in the studio.

**Reflected light and incident light**

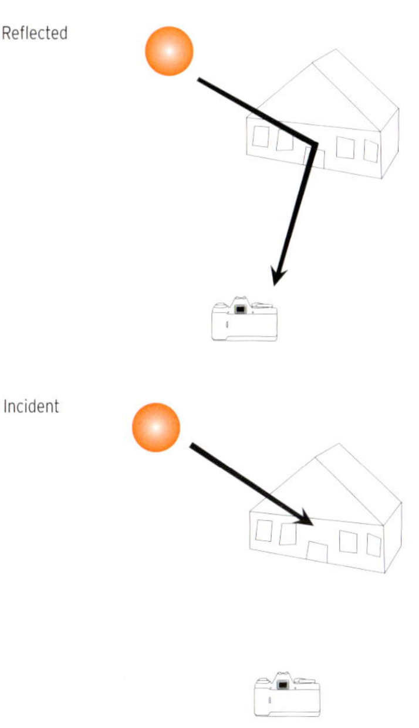


Meters that are built into cameras measure reflected light. An incident light meter measures the light actually falling on the subject.

## What is a grey card?

A grey card is simply a piece of card that is exactly 18% medium-grey in colour. It is used to take a light reading from a medium-toned subject when no natural subject is available.

## When would I use an incident light meter?

Incident light meters are excellent when the lighting conditions are complex. For example, they are traditionally used at weddings where the bride and groom typically wear white and black respectively.

# ENHANCING FILTERS AND PHOTOGRAPHIC FILTERS

## What do enhancing filters do?

Enhancing filters add in some way to existing lighting conditions. For example, a sepia-toned filter will alter a grey sky to make it appear orange-brown. Another example would be a blue graduated filter that enhances the colour of a blue sky while leaving foreground objects unchanged. Enhancement filters are typically coloured and work by altering the balance of the coloured light waves entering the lens. For example, a blue filter will block red and, to a lesser extent, green light waves, making blue the prevalent colour.

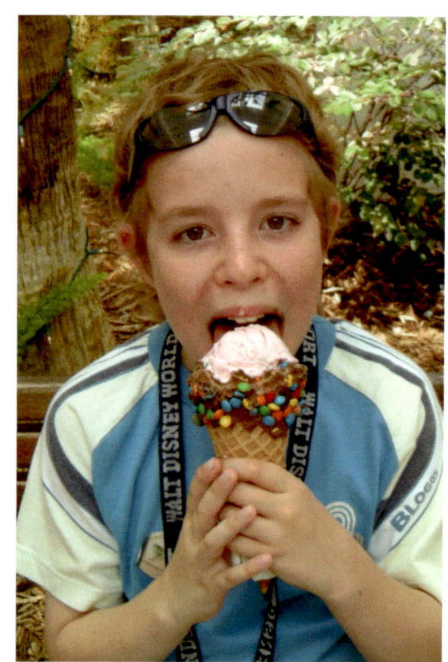


## When would I use enhancing filters?

Some traditionalists may argue that you shouldn't, in the same way they argue that computer-based image processing is cheating. There is no harm in using enhancing filters, such as those described, when a subtle increase or alteration of colour enhances the overall image, for example by increasing the vividness of a blue sky or adding interest to an otherwise dull sky.

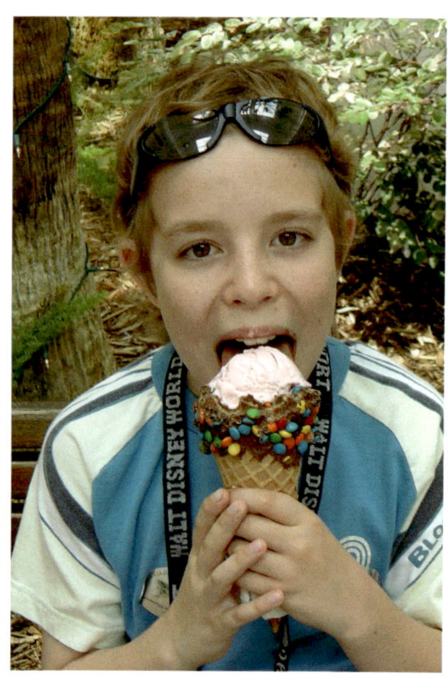


Enhancement filters, such as that used in the first shot (top) have the ability to enhance the warm colours in the scene (here most visible in the skin tone) without having so dramatic an effect on other colours. Compare this with a warming filter, for example, where greens and blues in the scene would be compromised by a warm colour cast.

## What types of enhancing filters are available?

There are a range of enhancing filters available on the market and they can be used for a wide variety of functions, such as to warm or cool an image, or to apply a tint. Each one has a specific use depending on the lighting conditions in which you are working. Some of the most commonly used enhancing filters and their functions are outlined below.

### Neutral density filters

Straight neutral density (ND) filters are used to reduce the overall amount of light entering the lens. Available in different strengths, typically from 1 to 3 stops in 0.5-stop increments, they are used to enable the use of slower shutter speeds when the intensity of light would otherwise be too great.

For example, say you wanted to photograph a waterfall and blur the motion of the water, which would require a shutter speed slower than 1/30 second. If the intensity of light is such that the slowest shutter speed attainable is, say, 1/125 second then the intensity of light would need reducing by at least 2 stops to achieve the 1/30 second shutter speed necessary. This would be possible by adding a 2-stop strength ND filter.

**See also**

*Filters for managing contrast (page 46)*

**Tip**

*When using neutral density filters and a non-TTL meter, it is important to remember to take into account the light-absorbing strength of the filter, and to adjust the exposure accordingly.*

### Ultraviolet filters

Ultraviolet (UV) filters are used to reduce the level of ultraviolet light entering the lens. UV light is invisible to the human eye but is recorded by photographic film and, to a lesser extent, digital sensors. It is strongest at high altitude and close to the coast. They are sometimes used also as protection for the front element of the lens. When this is the case, use the best-quality filter that you can afford because filters will affect image quality.

**See also**

*Visible light (page 14)*

### Skylight filters

Skylight filters are often used in place of UV filters. However, a true UV filter has no effect on colour while a skylight filter often produces a pink colour cast. Unless this is the effect you are specifically trying to achieve, stick to using UV filters, even when using them simply to protect the front element of the lens.

# CORRECTION FILTERS

### What do correction filters do?

Correction filters are used specifically to correct the inaccuracies that would be recorded by film or digital sensors relating to light in certain circumstances. For example, optical filters are used to correctly balance colour temperature, typically with film. And colour correction (CC) filters are used, among other things, to compensate for colour shifts that occur during, for example, long time exposures when using film.

### When would I use correction filters?

The most common correction filters are those used for balancing the colour temperature of light with film. These include the 81-series of orange filters that compensate for blue colour casts, and the 82-series of blue filters that compensate for red-orange colour casts. The table below also identifies some of the principal colour correction filters used to compensate for colour shifts when using certain film types.

### What does a yellow filter do in black-and-white photography?

Yellow or yellow/green filters are used in black-and-white photography to record grey tones much closer to their visual brightness than is recorded by black-and-white film. The difference is often minimal but can be essential in certain fields of technical photography where an accurate record of grey tones is necessary.

The principal colour correction filters

| Colour | Name | Effect |
| --- | --- | --- |
| | Cyan | Filter absorbs red |
| | Yellow | Filter absorbs blue |
| | Magenta | Filter absorbs green |
| | Red | Filter absorbs blue and green |
| | Green | Filter absorbs red and blue |
| | Blue | Filter absorbs red and green |

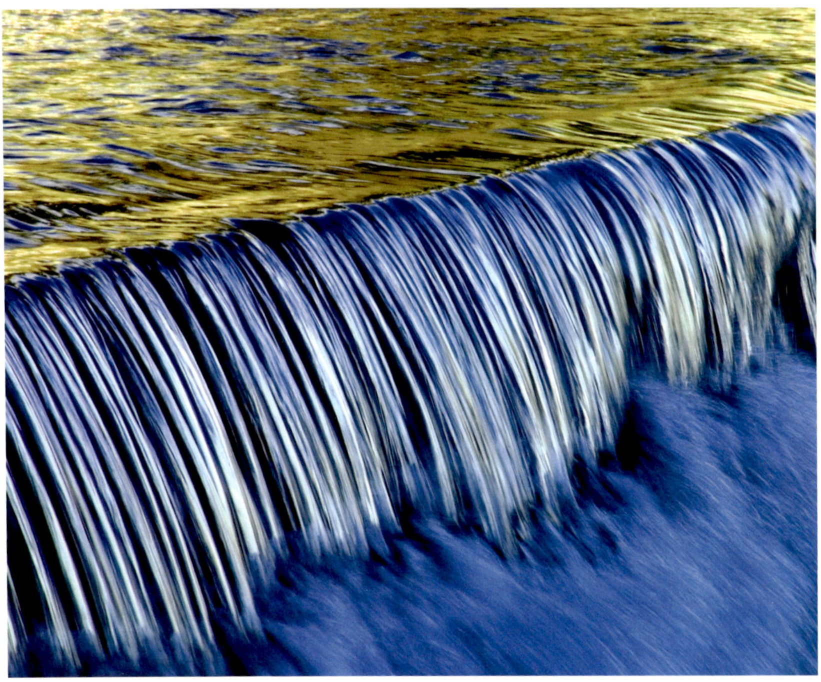

A polarising filter has helped to saturate and enhance the colours in this image of a weir in France.

### What does a polarising filter do?

Non-polarised light, which exists all around us, is what causes reflections to appear on shiny non-metallic surfaces, such as water and glass. It is also very apparent in light from a blue sky at right angles to the sun. Humans can't differentiate between polarised and non-polarised light but film and sensors can, and record it.

A polarising filter polarises non-polarised light, removing (or lessening at least) the reflections caused by non-polarised light, and darkens blue skies, increasing contrast between the sky and any clouds in the scene.

### What's the difference between a circular polariser and a linear polariser?

The two types of polarising filter affect light in the same way but linear polarisers will adversely affect the operation of auto-focus and auto-exposure systems in cameras. Therefore, if you are using a modern SLR or DSLR camera then it is recommended to use only a circular polariser.

# FILTERS FOR MANAGING CONTRAST

## What is a neutral density graduated (NDG) filter?

If you look at a NDG filter you'll notice that half of it is clear and half grey. The grey half blocks light from entering the lens, the exact amount dependent on the filter's strength. The purpose of these filters is to create a more even balance between light and dark tones in a scene, particularly where the range of tones exceeds the latitude of the film or sensor used.

For example, take a landscape scene where there is a large area of brightly lit sky and an equal area of foreground in shadow. The extent of the contrast in this scene may be too great for the film or sensor to record detail in both the highlights and shadows. By using a NDG filter to block light from the brightest area of the scene, in this case the sky, the tonal range falls within the film/sensor latitude and detail is retained overall.

A perfect NDG filter has no effect on colour balance and blocks all wavelengths equally. Some less expensive products, however, produce a slight colour cast.

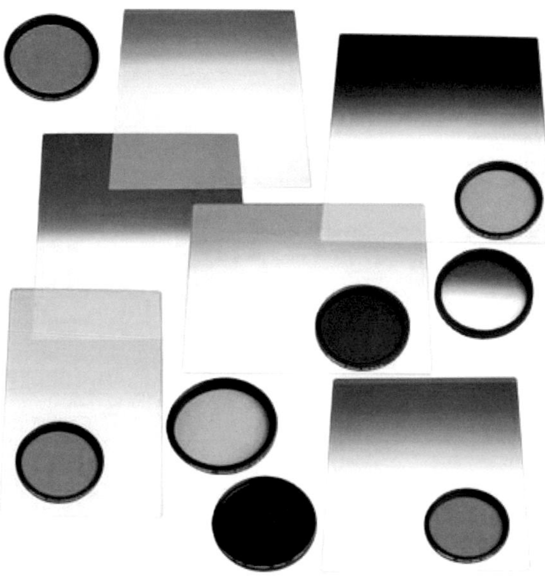

Graduated filters are available with different gradients and also different sizes to ensure coverage of all lens sizes. They are also available in conventional filter mounts and can be used with neutral density filters and/or polarising filters to get the desired effect.

## What do the numbers on NDG filters mean?

NDG filters come in different strengths, typically identified by a number, such as 0.3, 0.6 and 0.9. These numbers relate to stops of light. For example, a 0.3 NDG blocks 1 stop of light, a 0.6 NDG blocks 2 stops of light, and so on. The full range of neutral density filter strengths is from 0.15 (half-stop), 0.3, 0.45, 0.6, 0.75, 0.9, to 1.2 (4 stops).

### What is the difference between a hard NDG filter and a soft one?

With a soft NDG filter the change between clear and grey is gradual, leading to a less pronounced effect. With hard NDG filters the change between clear and grey is immediate, with no gradual darkening, which gives a more pronounced effect.

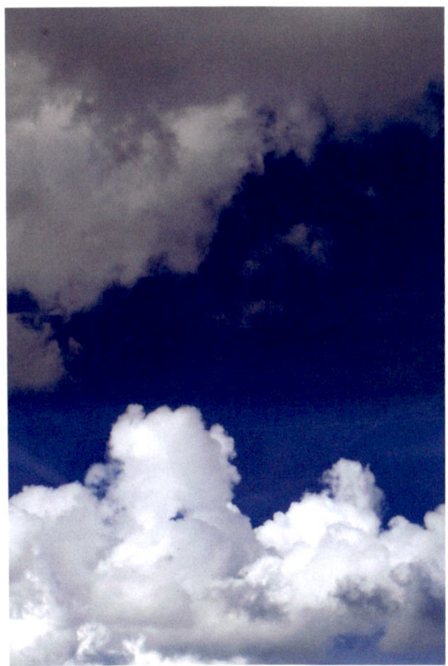

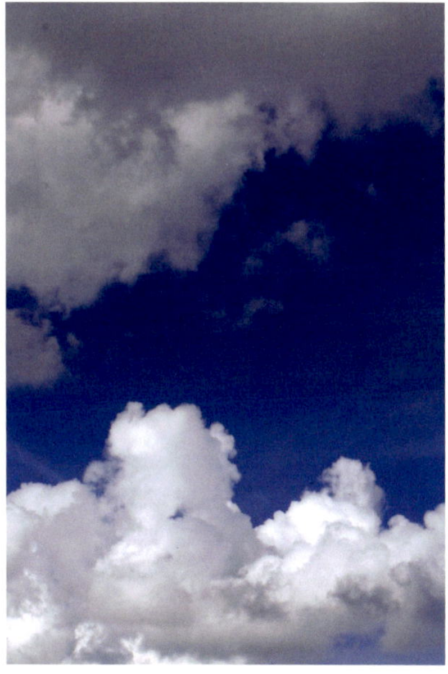

These two images have both been taken using a NDG filter. The image on the left has been taken with a hard NDG filter, and the contrast can be seen. The image on the right has been taken with a soft NDG filter, hence the contrast is more gradual.

### How do coloured filters work in black-and-white photography?

Black-and-white film is very sensitive to blue light with the result that a clear blue sky will appear paler than it appears to the eye and contrast between the sky and any clouds visible is diminished.

A red filter absorbs blue light with the effect of darkening the blue colour of the sky and increasing contrast between dark and light tones. An orange filter has a similar effect although less pronounced than when using a red filter.

Red and orange filters are less effective on overcast days and can be too effective when used to photograph scenes with a predominance of other colours. For example, a scene that contains a large area of green, a forest of trees for instance, would result in both the sky and trees darkening if a red filter was used. However, a green filter will lighten the leaves while still adding density to the blue sky.

# LENS HOODS

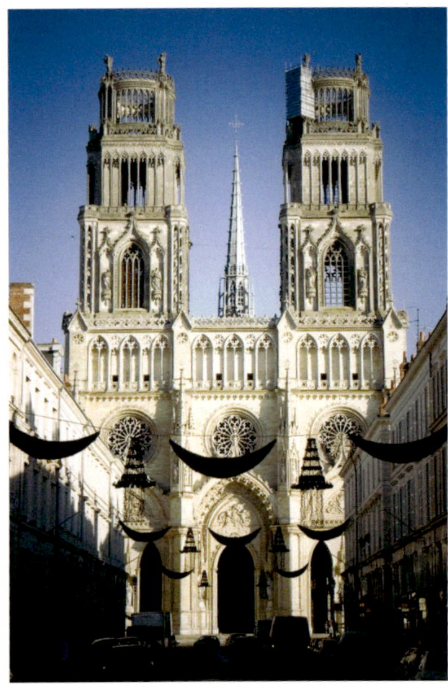

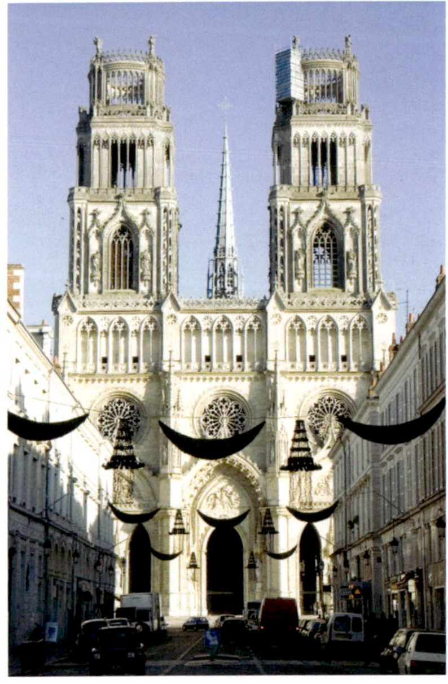

## Why do I need a lens hood?

Lens hoods are underrated camera accessories. Their main function is to prevent the occurrence of lens flare, which can ruin an otherwise successful image. They also help to protect the front element of the lens from rain and dirt.

## Can I use the same lens hood on any lens?

There are some generic lens hoods designed to fit a range of lenses and for lenses within a focal range of 50-200mm these are generally suitable. However, care should be taken when working with wide-angle and long telephoto lenses, the two types of lenses most affected by lens flare. The angle of view of a wide-angle lens is often so great that an inappropriate lens hood will appear in the picture, causing vignetting (dark areas at the corners of the image space). With long telephoto lenses the lens hoods need to be deep enough to prevent light scatter, one of the causes of flare. Most new lenses come with a custom lens hood and it is advisable to use this with the relevant lens.

Using an appropriate lens hood can cause vignetting. It is advisable to use the custom-designed lens hoods available for most lenses.

### What is a panel reflector?

Panel reflectors are used to balance light and moderate areas of shadow, acting much like fill-flash by adding light to areas of a scene unlit by the main light source. They are typically coloured white, silver or gold, each having a slightly different effect, and there is also a black reflector, which is used to absorb light. Panel reflectors are used often in portrait photography, both outdoors and in the studio. Typically positioned directly opposite the main light and close to the subject, they provide subtle fill light to the model's face or body. The advantage of panel reflectors is that they can never be brighter than the primary light source, which means they will never overpower the main light.

**See also**

*Artificial studio lighting (page 128)*

A reflector (in the photographer's hand) helps to shine light back on to the subject.

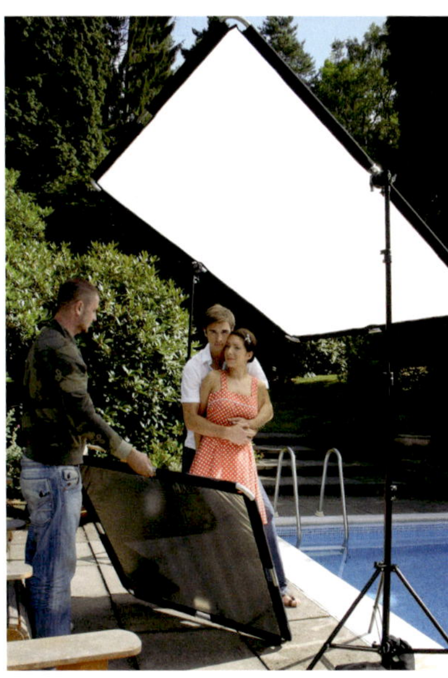

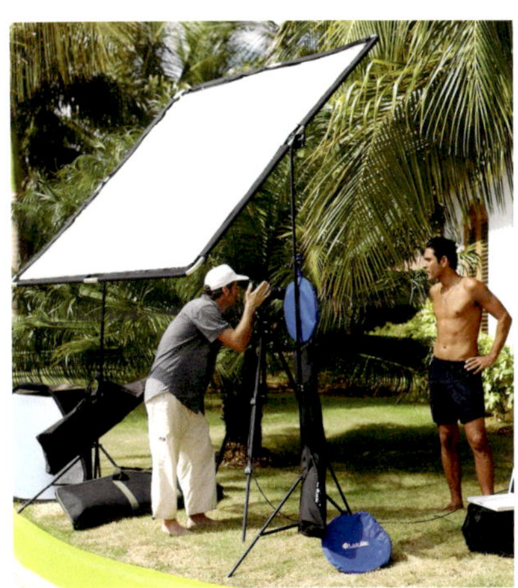

A diffuser will soften hard, directional lighting.

### What is a diffuser?

Whether outdoors or in a studio, diffusers are used to create soft (omni-directional) lighting from a point light source. Made from white nylon (or from any semi-transparent material), placed between the light source and the subject, the diffuser scatters light, creating a softer quality. Coloured diffusers can also be used although the diffused light will take on the colour of the diffuser.

**See also**

*Quality of light (page 24)*

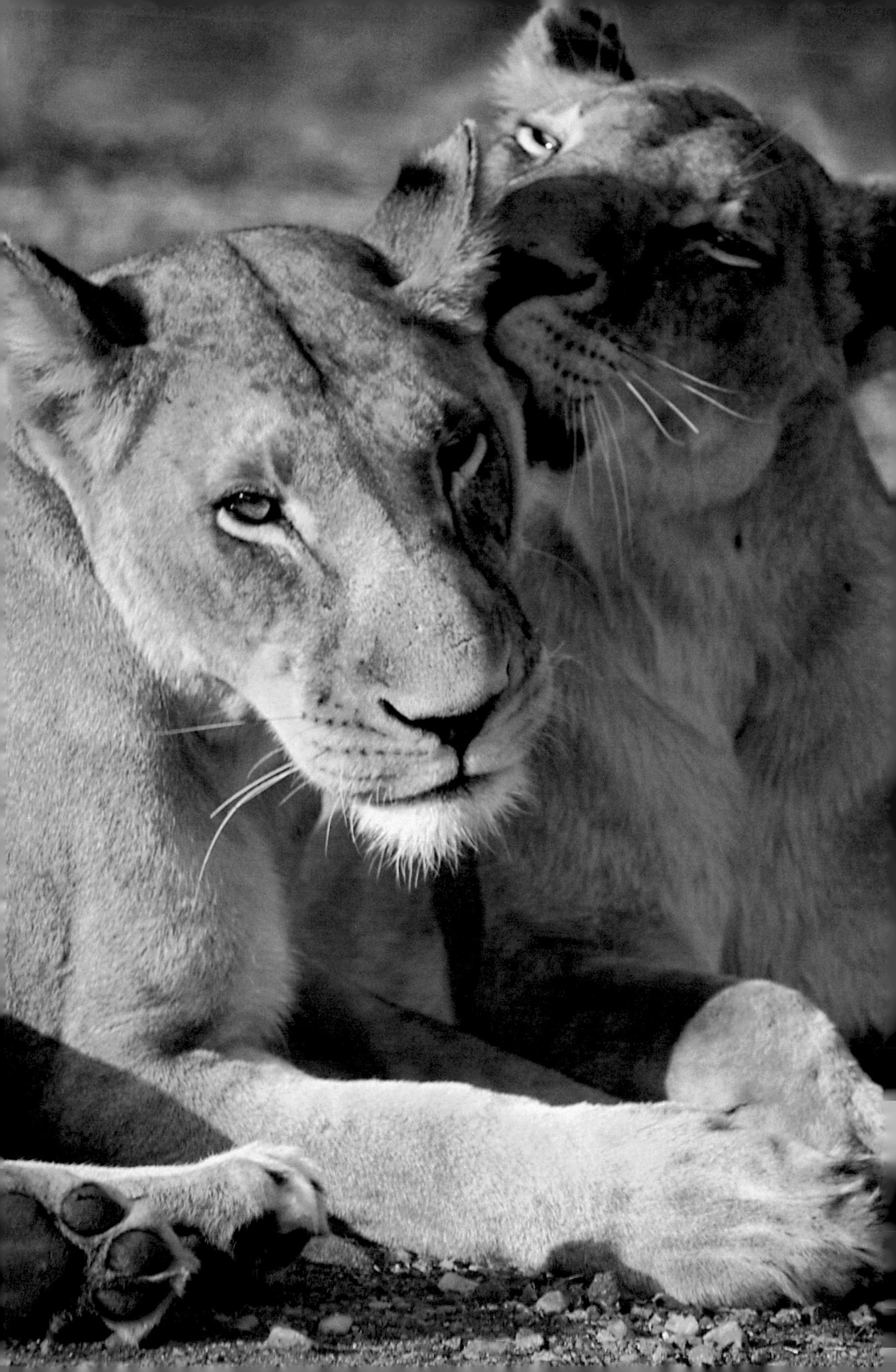

SECTION THREE
# NATURAL LIGHT

The art of photography has everything to do with light and there is nothing to match the beauty and photographic quality of natural light. Recognising 'the sweet light' and knowing how to manipulate it is the most important job a photographer does. Understanding the effects on light of the time of day, weather and seasonal variations will enable you to predict light patterns and anticipate when and where to be with your camera. The following section will help you build your knowledge of and skills in exploiting natural light.



Being able to recognise 'the sweet light' is one of the most important photographic skills you will learn.

# 15 NATURAL LIGHT
## THE TIME OF DAY

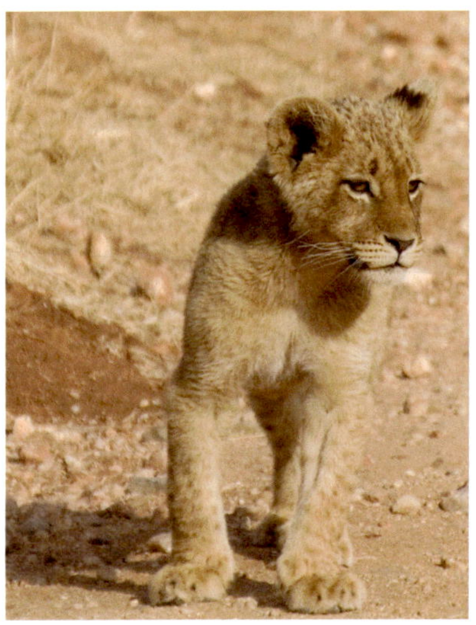

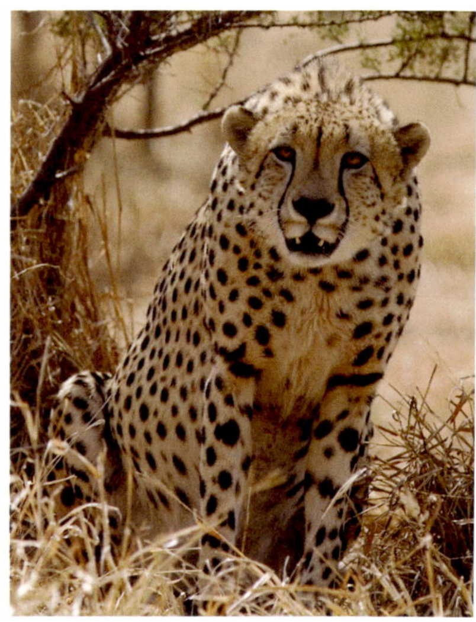

In the early morning light comes from the side (when light is direct), creating long shadows (left). Later in the day, shadows are shorter (right).

### How does light change throughout the day?

The obvious difference in sunlight as time passes is its position in the sky. At sunrise the sun is at 90° until around mid-day when, depending on the time of year and subject to geography, it is typically overhead. This movement is reversed as the clock ticks through to sunset. Two less obvious changes caused by this movement occur during the day. Firstly, the length of shadows decreases as the sun rises - in the early morning shadows are long, elongated; secondly the colour temperature of light alters from red (sunrise/sunset) to blue-white (noon). This latter change is almost invisible to humans because our brains perform a kind of White Balance control that ensures we see all light as neutral white light.

### How do these changes affect my photography?

The answer to this question is in two parts. The presence of shadows is what gives an image form. At noon in summertime, when ground shadows are almost non-existent, objects in an image will seem flat. The same object photographed earlier in the day will have shadows that highlight contours (e.g. in the landscape or a person's face) and the angled surfaces of buildings, creating a three-dimensional appearance.

**See also**

*Quality of light (page 24)*

### Why is colour temperature important?

Colour temperature is important because, while our brains adjust for colour casts caused by colour temperature, cameras do not. Film and digital sensors record light exactly as it appears unless a compensation factor is applied.

As an example, if you take a photograph indoors using light from a household light bulb with daylight-balanced film, the resulting image will have a stark orange colour cast, caused by the low colour temperature of light from the bulb compared to high-angled sunlight.

This is an extreme example but subtle colour casts are apparent unless the film/sensor is balanced to match exactly the colour temperature of the prevailing light. With film, this balancing act is performed using colour filters and in digital photography via the White Balance control.

**See also**

*Colour temperature (page 17)*
*Enhancing filters and photographic filters (page 42)*

### How do colour filters and digital White Balance work?

Colour filters are used in conjunction with film. For example, since the colour temperature of light in the early morning has an orange cast, using a blue filter will reduce the amount of red light entering the lens, which, in turn, will nullify the orange cast. Conversely, if there is a preponderance of blue light (typically around midday), an orange filter will better balance the level of red light, creating a more natural effect.

White Balance is used in digital cameras to match the balance of the sensor with the Kelvin temperature of the light. In this way it is possible to compensate for colour casts exactly. In practice a close match is sufficient in most circumstances and can be performed by using one of the camera's pre-set WB settings (see table). Auto-WB will attempt to perform an exact match based on through-the-lens data (and, in the case of the Nikon D2Xs and D2Hs cameras, incident light data) in much the same way that a TTL-AE system tries to calculate an accurate exposure. In some cases this works well but may not produce the effect you're trying to create. In any case, unlike optical filters, the effect of any camera-set WB setting can be altered during the RAW conversion stage, if the original file is shot in RAW mode.

White Balance settings

| WB setting | Use |
|---|---|
| Daylight | Late morning to early afternoon through noon on a sunny day. |
| Cloudy | Overcast conditions. Can also be used to add warmth to landscape scenes in much the same way as using an 81-series filter. |
| Shade | When subject is in heavy shade. |
| Incandescent (tungsten) | When a tungsten light (e.g. a household light bulb) is the primary light source. |
| Fluorescent | When fluorescent lighting is the primary light source. |
| Flash | When electronic flash is the primary light source. The Flash setting is very close to the Daylight setting. |

# THE WEATHER

## How does weather affect light quality?

Think of the sun as a studio flash head. Unobstructed sunlight is directional (a point source) in the same way that an unobstructed flash is directional. The light from a directional, point source is typically hard, creating prominent shadows. Now put a soft box over our hypothetical studio flash and the light becomes much softer. Cloud cover has the same effect on sunlight, producing much softer (omni-directional) light and less well-defined shadows. So, direct sunlight is considered hard in quality and diffused sunlight is soft in quality.

We often think of photography in terms of bright, sunny conditions but photography doesn't have to be a fair-weather pursuit. This image was taken on a wet, miserable winter morning and the quality of light has added to the composition in a positive way.

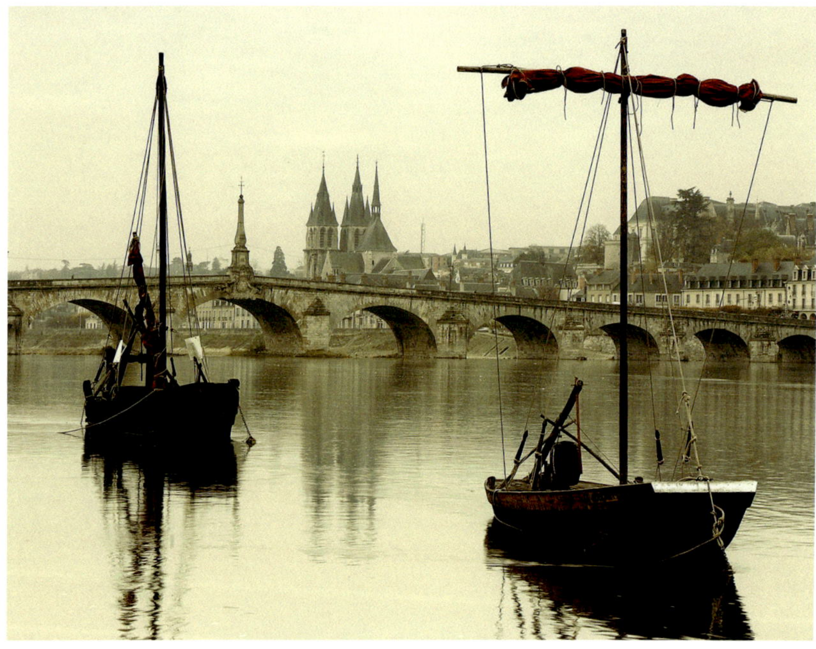

**See also**

*Quality of light (page 24)*

## How does the quality of light affect my photography?

Direct light from a point source (hard light) has the effect of increasing contrast, which makes it harder for the camera to record detail in highlight and shadow areas simultaneously. Hard light also darkens and better defines shadows, making them more prominent in the picture. Omni-directional light from a diffused source (soft light) reduces contrast, making it easier for the camera to record detail across a wide tonal range, and softening the appearance of shadows.

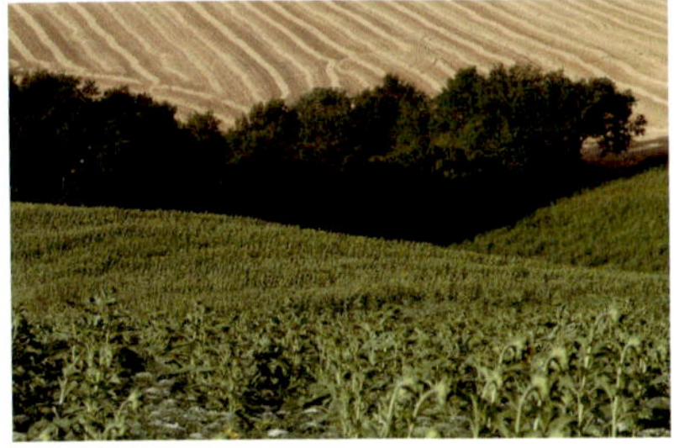
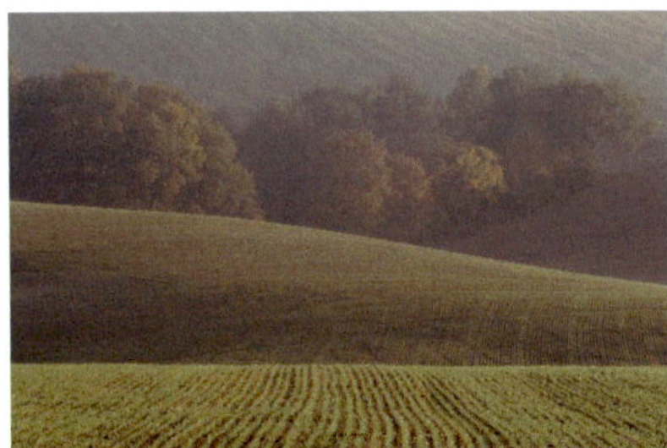
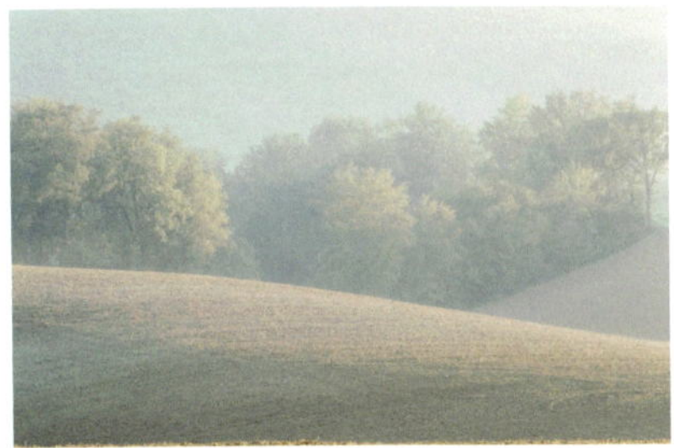

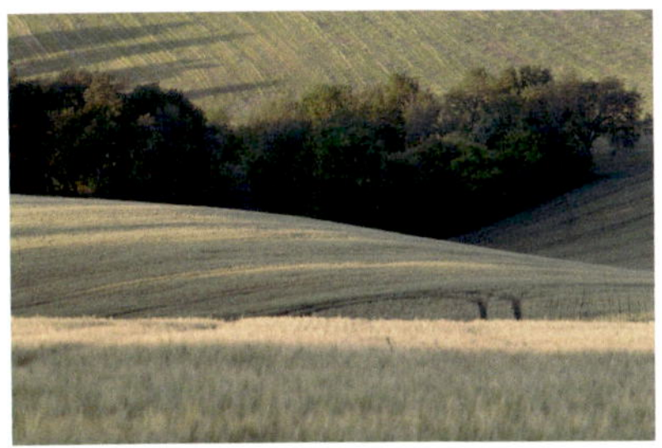
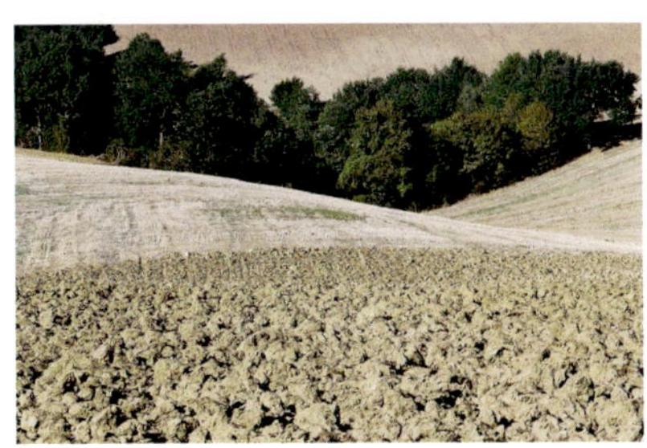

Both changes in season and the time of day can dramatically change the same landscape.

### How does light change throughout the seasons?

The obvious answer to this question is you get more light for longer in summer than you do in winter. While this is true there is a more important difference in light between the seasons. In late spring and summertime the sun rises high in the sky, to a point when it is directly overhead. However, during late autumn and winter the sun never reaches this lofty peak and even at midday it is at a more acute angle.

### How do seasonal changes in light affect my photography?

The effect of the angle of sunlight is to create and increase the length of shadows. Shadows, in the form of contrast, are what give an image its form, or three-dimensional appearance. Shadowless scenes appear flat on paper, losing this increased sense of three dimensions.

## How can I exploit the colour temperature of light?

While we all see the world as if it was lit by neutral white light, sometimes we want to perceive it differently. For example, imagine a picture of a sunrise or sunset that had all of the brilliant, warm red/orange light removed! In its simplest form, managing colour temperature will exploit humans' emotional responses to colours. For instance, as warm-blooded creatures we like, indeed need, to feel warmth, and respond positively to warm colours, such as red, orange and yellow. Conversely, when we expect to feel cold, e.g. in the presence of snow and ice, a warm colour cast will appear unnatural and blue, a cold colour, will give an image a more natural feel.

Optical filters of the 81-series (warming filters) and 80-series (cooling filters) can be used to alter the apparent colour temperature to create natural-looking colour casts. For example, landscape photographers often shoot with an 81A- or 81B-series filter in order to 'warm' their images of natural scenery.

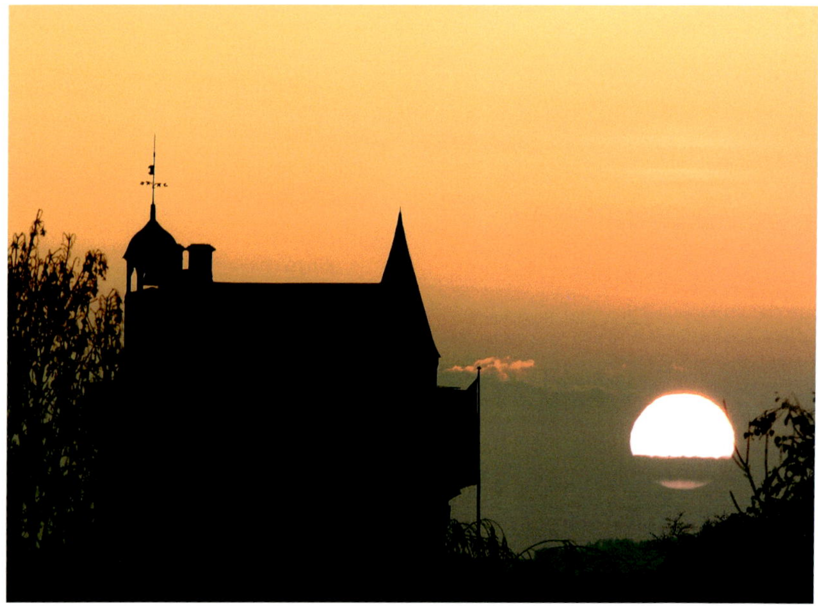

The golden hours of sunrise and sunset are a prime example of how photographers can exploit changes in the colour temperature of light.

**See also**

*Equipment and camera functions (page 32)*

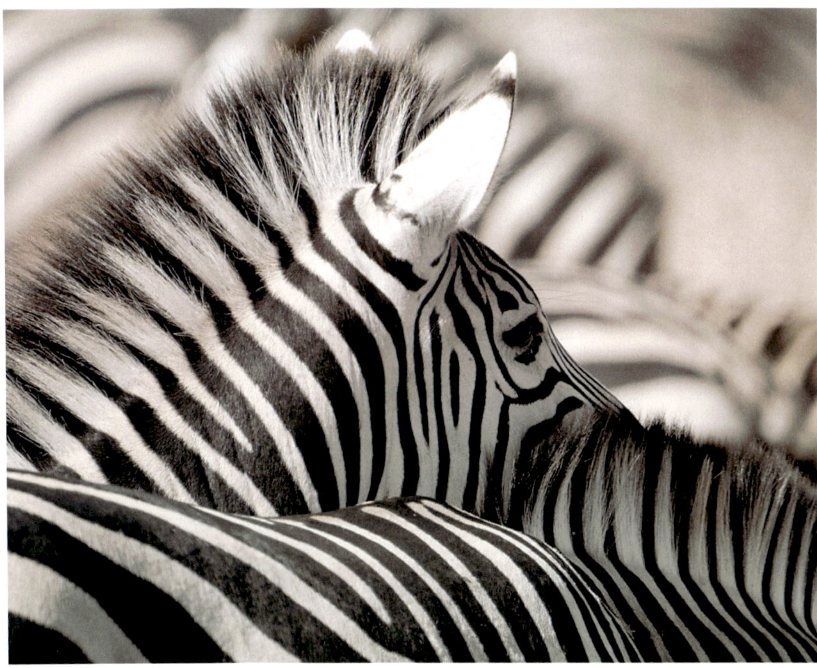

This image of zebras would have been impossible if the light had been hard and direct. By photographing on an overcast day, the softer quality of light has brought the level of contrast to within the dynamic range of the sensor allowing detail to be recorded in both the highlight and shadow areas.

## How can I benefit from diffused light?

Diffused light reduces contrast and makes it easier to photograph scenes with a wide tonal range while maintaining detail in both shadow and highlight areas. For example, think about a wedding scene: the bride dressed in a white dress of delicate, finely detailed fabric, the groom in a black suit. On a sunny day the tonal range would be too great for a camera to be able to record detail in both the dress and the suit simultaneously. However, on a cloudy day, when the light is diffused and levels of contrast are reduced, the tonal range is more likely to fall within the latitude of the film or sensor, making it possible to capture detail in both the black-and-white tonal extremes.

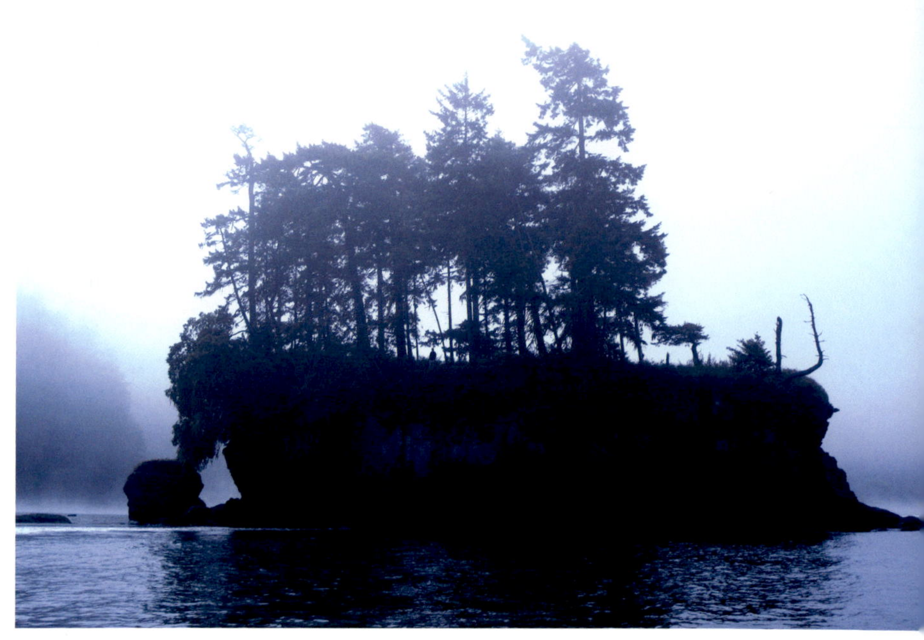

## How do I cope with excessive contrast?

When contrast extends beyond the latitude of film or the digital sensor (referred to as dynamic range) it may be possible to control or adjust the level or quality of light entering the lens. For example, if the subject allows, a studio diffuser can be employed outside to soften the light specific to the subject. This is often possible in macro photography, where the subject is small enough to allow the use of a diffuser.

It is also possible with neutral density graduated filters to adjust the quantity of light reaching the film from a selected portion of the scene. For example, the tonal balance between a bright sky and a foreground in shadow can be made even by placing the dark portion of the NDG filter over the lens so that it corresponds to the area of sky that can be seen in the frame.

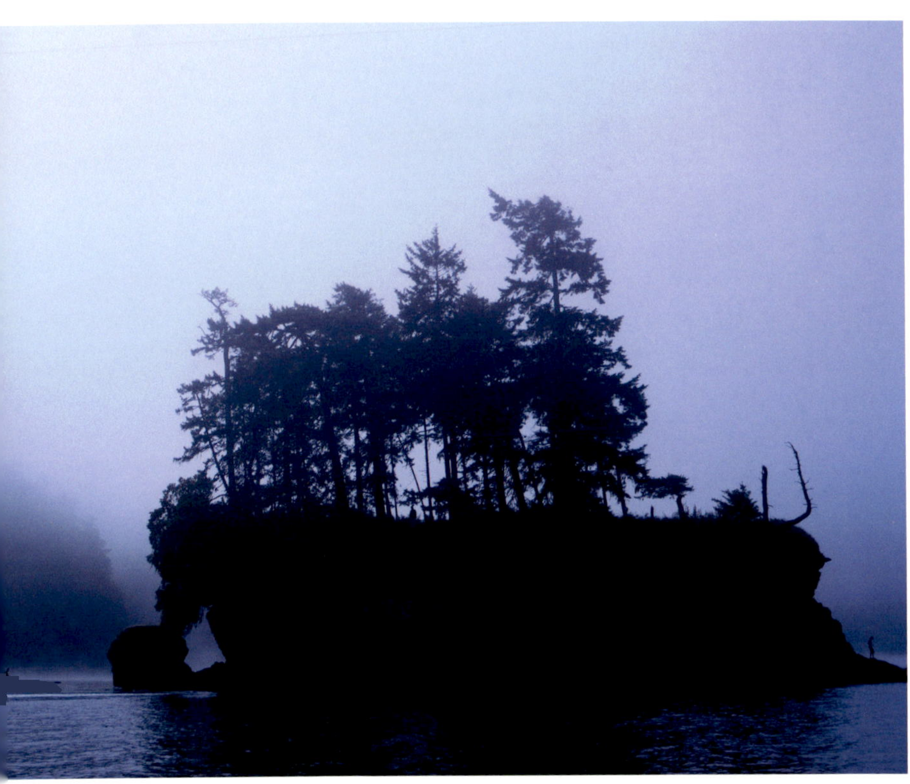

Another option is to use fill-in flash to 'throw' light into the shadow areas. This has the effect of reducing contrast by narrowing the tonal range.

Also, when shooting in weather that includes broken clouds, it may be appropriate to wait until a moment when a passing cloud obscures the sun (diffusing its light) before making the image.

A neutral density graduated filter has been used to moderate the intensity of light falling on the film/sensor, overcoming the limitations of narrow latitude/dynamic range.

**See also**

*Filters for managing contrast (page 46)*
*Using fill-in flash with natural light (page 66)*
*Natural light (page 50)*

### How do I deal with backlighting?

The main issue with backlighting is that it leaves the camera-facing portion of the subject in shadow while lighting the background, with the obvious result that, unless dealt with carefully, the background becomes the subject and the original subject is figuratively lost in the shadows.

There are two main methods of dealing with backlighting. You can expose for the subject by taking a selective meter reading (i.e. a spot-meter reading) from the subject directly and using this as your exposure. This will create a halo of light around the subject, which can be aesthetically appealing. Alternatively, you can meter for the background so rendering the subject widely under-exposed and in silhouette. Used well and appropriately silhouettes produce images with very strong graphic appeal.

Another option is to apply fill-in flash to light the subject and allowing the natural light to light the background. Used effectively, a natural balance between daylight and natural light can be achieved.

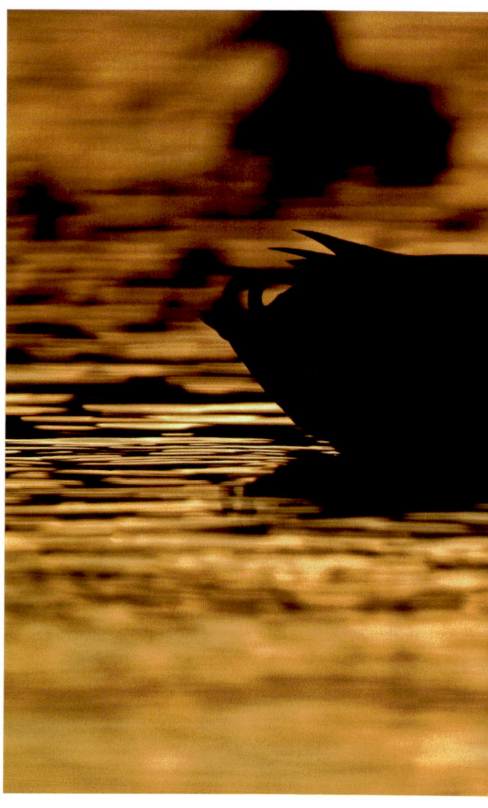

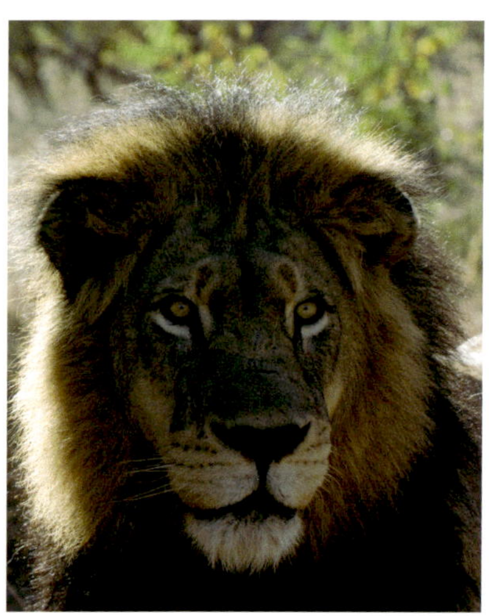

How you expose for backlighting will determine the outcome of the image. By exposing for the background highlights you can create evocative silhouettes, as in the first image (above). Alternatively, exposing for the shadow areas in the foreground will produce a halo of rim light, as in the second image (left).

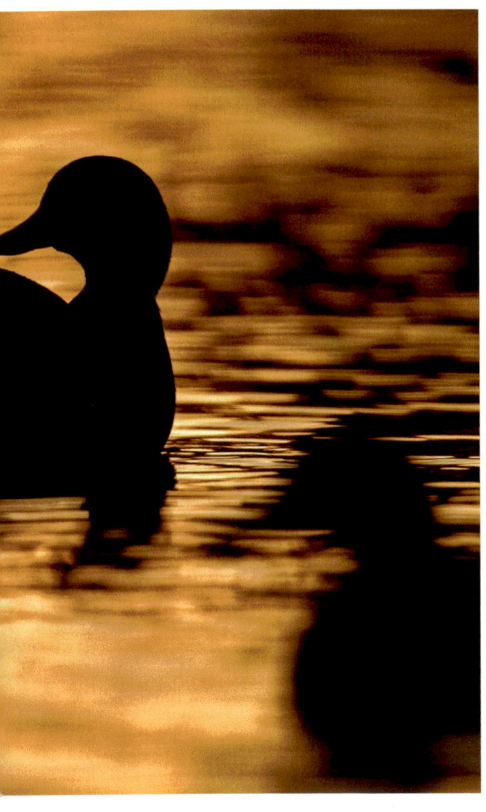

### See also

*Using fill-in flash with natural light (page 66)*

### Tip

*When shooting into the sun it is advisable to attach a lens shade to the front of the lens to help avoid lens flare appearing on the image.*

### Why would I want to change the quality of light?

Changing the quality of light from a hard to soft source, or vice versa, alters the level of contrast within a scene. Soft lighting will reduce levels of contrast while hard lighting will increase it. By adjusting the source of light between hard and soft you can manage contrast.

### How can I affect the quality of light outdoors?

The problem with outdoor photography is that you have no control over weather, which ultimately affects the quality of light. However, in a limited way, it's possible to change light quality even outside. For example, a large diffuser can be placed between the sunlight falling on a subject and the subject itself, which will soften the quality of the light falling on the subject. Of course, without help from an artificial source, it's very difficult to create hard light from soft light, but flash can be used to for this purpose.

### See also

*Quality of light (page 24)*

### When is front lighting most appropriate?

Front lighting is most appropriate when your aim is to highlight features and details, as opposed to texture and form. For example, if you are trying to record the features of a building without any interest in the texture of the material used to build it, then front lighting would be appropriate.

# 20 NATURAL LIGHT

## CHANGING THE COLOUR TEMPERATURE OF NATURAL LIGHT

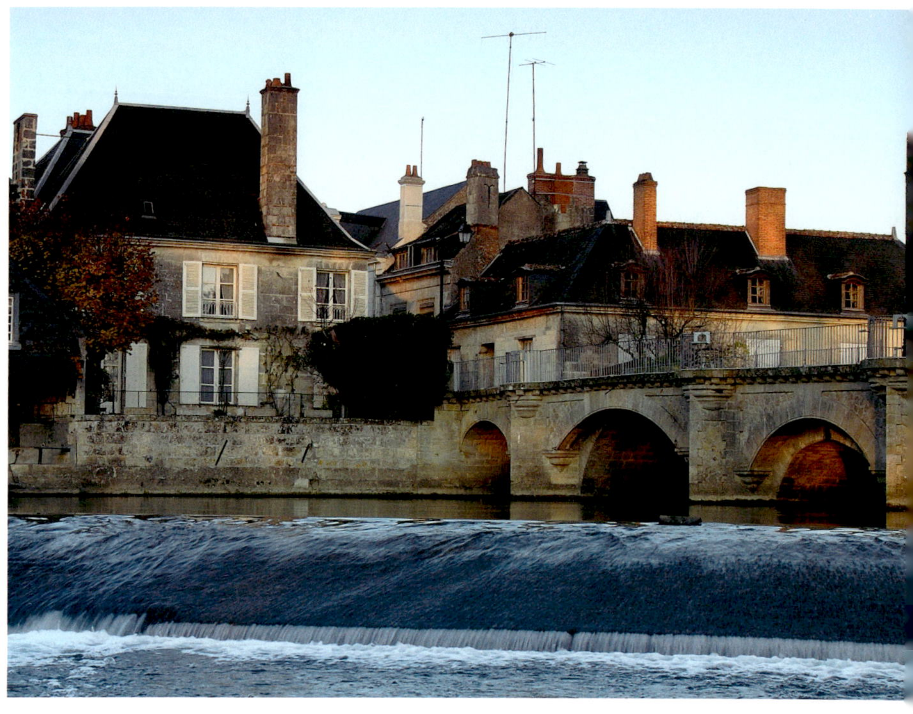

### Why would I want to change the colour temperature of natural light?

There are two main reasons for changing the colour temperature of light entering the lens: firstly for technical reasons (creating natural white light from a non-white light source) or, secondly, for artistic reasons, for example to make the light in a scene appear warmer or cooler.

An example of a technical application would be when shooting a sports event in a stadium under fluorescent-type lighting. Without compensating for the colour temperature images will have an unnatural green colour cast, caused by the colour temperature of fluorescent lighting. Compensating for this colour cast using either filters or the White Balance setting on digital cameras will produce a more natural result equivalent to our own vision.

An artistic example would be using an 81-series 'warm' filter when photographing in dense forest, where the heavy level of shade coupled with an expanse of green foliage would greatly increase the level of blue light entering the lens. Using an orange filter would give the scene a warmer, more appealing feel.

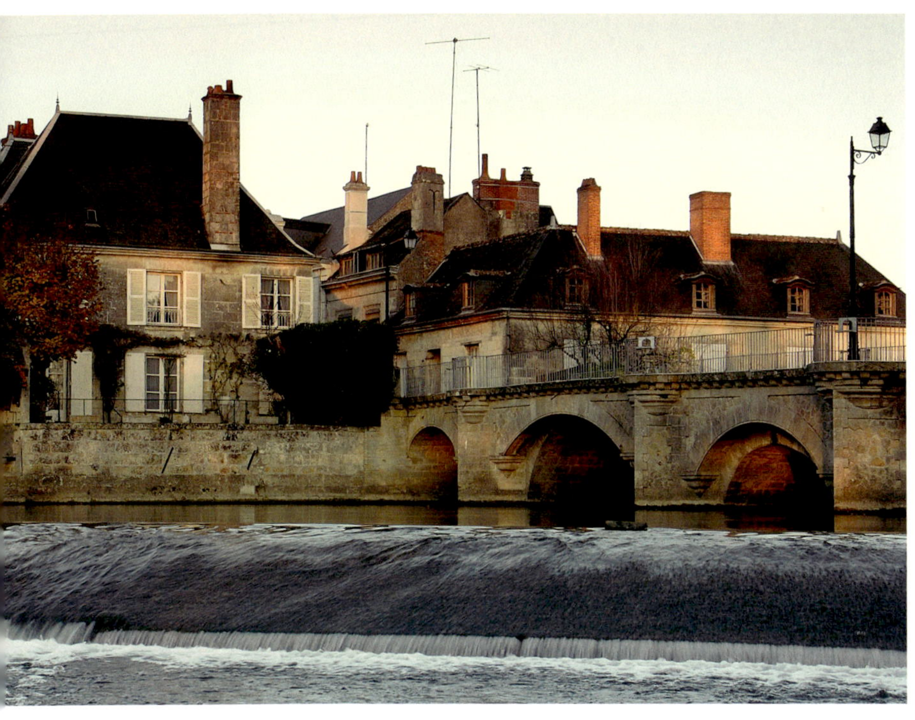

## When would I not want to adjust colour temperature?

If the image is a record shot and the intention is to accurately record colours, such as when photographing fashion or product shots, then it's important that colours are reproduced naturally.

These two comparative images show how compensating for colour temperature can alter the emotional response to an image. The first image (left) shows a neutral balance and is close to how the scene appeared to the naked eye. For the second image (right) an 81A 'warm' filter was applied to add an orange colour cast, giving the image a warmer feel.

### Tip

*When using optical filters with digital cameras it is important not to use the Auto-WB setting, as the camera will automatically compensate for any adjustments to colour temperature caused by the filter, so nullifying the filter's effect.*

### How can I affect the colour temperature of light outdoors?

With all camera types (film or digital), optical filters, such as those made by Hoya, Lee, Cokin and B&W, can be used to manipulate the light entering the lens. In digital photography the White Balance control on the camera can be used to set specific Kelvin values that affect the way the sensor reacts to light.

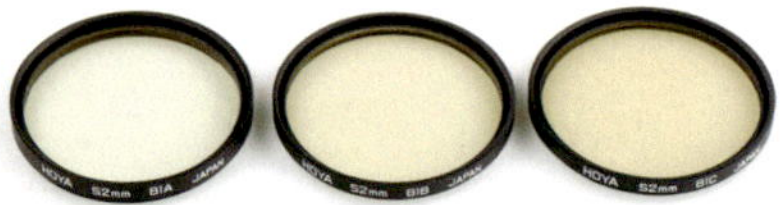

Optical filters – used to affect how the camera records light.

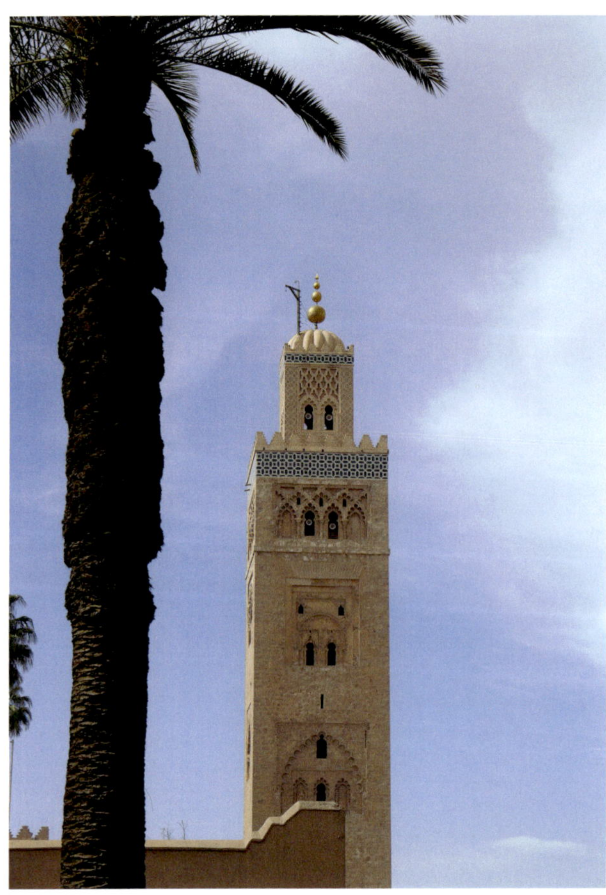

By setting the White Balance to a lower value (in this case to the Cloudy setting of around 3,200K) the cool blue cast in the first image (left) has been replaced with a warmer orange cast (right).

### Does setting WB matter if I'm shooting in RAW file mode?

It depends on how much work you want to do later on the computer. White Balance can be set at the RAW conversion stage of image processing, without any negative effect on image quality. However, any post-capture processing takes time and you may decide that it's better to get it right in camera, as it is one less thing to worry about later.

### What is the purpose of the pre-set WB setting?

When you are photographing under a consistent light source, such as in a studio, it is possible to measure the exact Kelvin value of the lighting and to set a specific WB value to match. When shooting outdoors under natural light, when the colour temperature of light can be changing constantly, calculating the exact Kelvin temperature is impossible for all practical purposes.

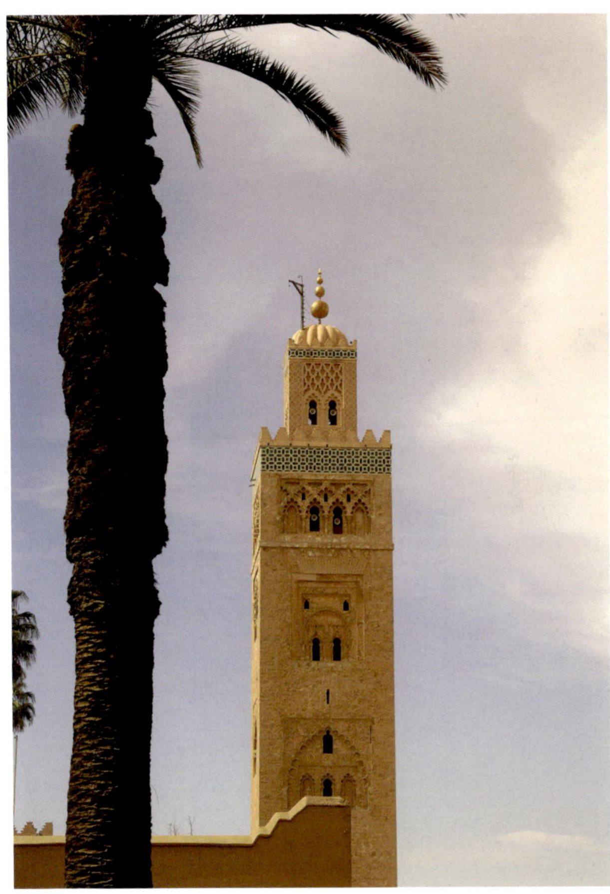

**See also**

*Filters for managing contrast (page 46)*

# USING FILL-IN FLASH WITH NATURAL LIGHT

### What is fill-in flash?

Simply put, fill-in flash is artificial light from a flash unit used to supplement natural light in order to increase illumination in shadow areas, thereby reducing contrast.

### When would I use fill-in flash?

Say you are photographing a model outdoors and the model's face is lit from the left side, as you view it from the camera. In this instance, half the model's face will be lit (the left half) while the right half will be in shadow.

If the sunlight is direct then the shadow will be intense and well-defined. By using flash light to light the right side of the model's face, the unlit side of the face will be better illuminated, reducing or eradicating shadows.

Another example where you might use fill-in flash is applicable to backlighting, where the whole of the subject facing the camera is unlit. To avoid creating a golden halo or silhouette effect (see page 60) fill-in flash can be used to light the subject.

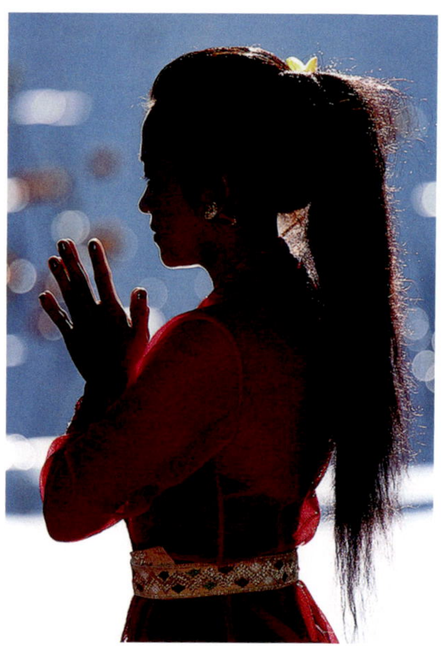

### How do I balance fill-in flash with ambient light for a natural look?

Modern dedicated flash units tend to have an automatic fill-in flash setting that can be used to balance flash output with the natural light. However, it is always useful to understand the manual method for such techniques, in case the camera gets it wrong.

To calculate the necessary flash output level, first take a meter reading for the area lit by natural light and note the EV. Then take a flash meter reading of the area lit with the flash and note the EV. The EV for the flash should be less than or equal to the EV for the natural light.

If the flash EV is greater then you will need to reduce manually the output of the flash. Where the two EVs are equal the level of light will be the same, which may result in a flat, formless image. Ideally, the EV for the flash should be around 0.5 – 1 stop lower than the EV for the ambient light, which will help to retain a level of contrast sufficient to maintain subject form.

### Can I use the pop-up flash on my camera for fill-in flash?

The built-in pop-up flash on the camera is useful for fill-in flash but it suffers from being positioned directly above the camera lens, which creates frontal and direct lighting. Diffusing the flash will soften shadows created by the direct source of light, and can help to reduce red-eye. However, there's little that can be done about the flash's position.

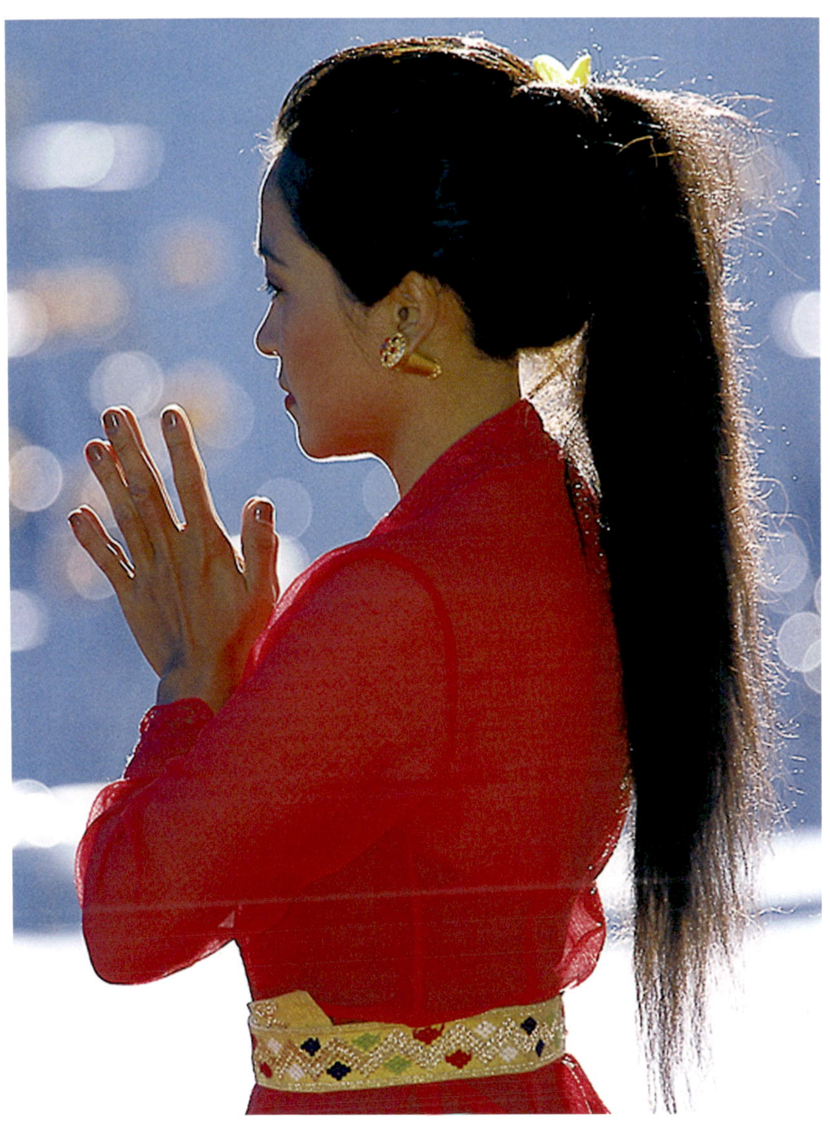

Fill-in flash has helped to lighten the shadows in this candid portrait image.

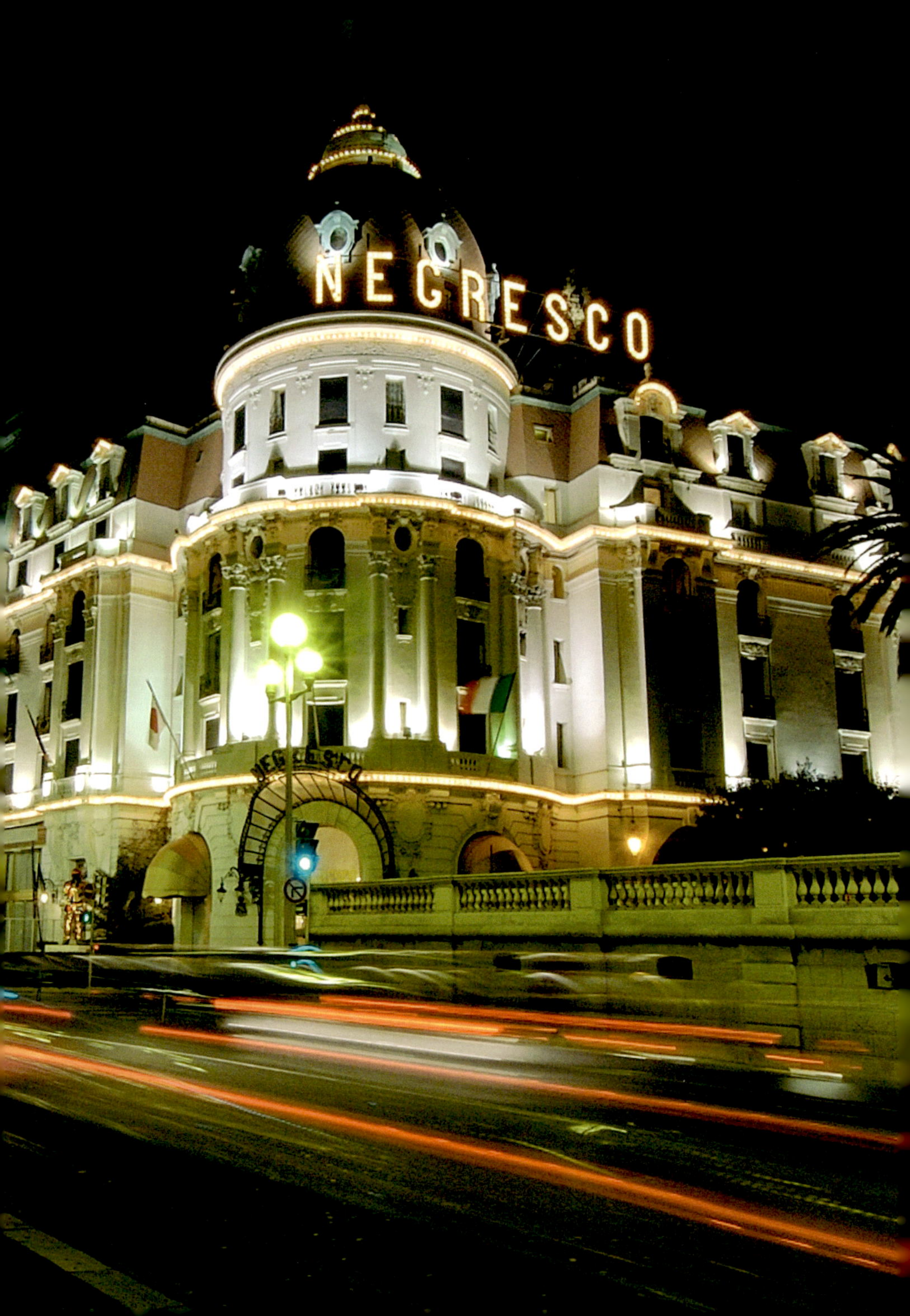
NEGRESCO

SECTION FOUR

# NIGHT AND LOW LIGHT

Photography doesn't have to stop when the sun goes down! The ethereal atmospheres of light at dusk and dawn, and soft moonlight, have a character and ambience all their own. Photographing during these low light hours can be fun and rewarding but does require some special skills, and you'll need to ensure your equipment is up to the job. The following section details how to prepare for and exploit the special quality of light at this time and explains how to capture unusual images of the outside world.



Photographic fun doesn't have to stop after the sun has gone down. Night photography is full of interesting and creative opportunities.

# WORKING IN LOW LIGHT

## What is considered low light?

This is a subjective point but typically the hours between dusk and dawn is the time of day we classify as low light. Of course, low light can happen at any time of the day when the weather conspires to block sunlight from reaching the landscape. Heavy cloud, fog and mist will all cause light levels to drop to a point where long shutter speeds become the norm.

## Do I need any special equipment when shooting in low light?

You can get by photographing in low light using standard photographic equipment but you will require some items that you may not normally use at other times.

Your camera must have a manual exposure mode and allow for setting slow shutter speeds via a Bulb or Time setting, which enables the shutter to be open for very long periods (often minutes or even hours). A mirror lock-up function is useful to help minimise camera shake and an input for a manual or electronic cable release is essential. You may find that many of the electronic, automated camera functions don't work properly in low light and that auto-exposure and auto-focus become pretty much redundant.

Away from the camera, you will need a sturdy tripod that is designed to hold the combined weight of your camera and lens, a manual or electronic cable release (if your cable release has no timer function, a watch with a second hand or a stop watch will be useful for counting long exposures), a torch to allow you to read easily the camera dials and settings, and spare batteries. If you are considering combining natural light and artificial light then a suitable flash unit will be needed, ideally one that can be held off-camera.

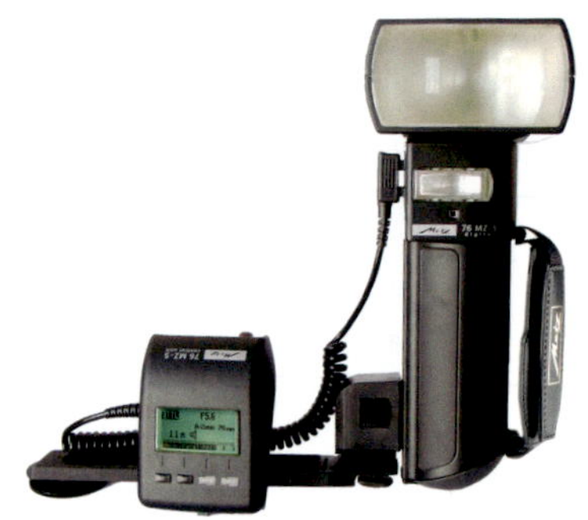

A hammerhead flash unit - the most powerful type of portable external flash guns - will give strong coverage and fast recycling times.

### How do I avoid camera shake and image blur?

Because it is most likely you will be using long time exposures a tripod will be essential. When using the tripod, keep its centre of gravity low and avoid using the centre column. In windy conditions, weight the tripod by hanging a weight from the bottom of the centre column. Shielding the camera in high winds will also help prevent camera movement during exposures. When using a tripod a cable release will avoid causing camera movement when triggering the shutter. An alternative is to use the self-timer to trigger the shutter but this isn't feasible when using the Bulb/Time setting. Finally, if your camera has it, use the mirror lock-up function.

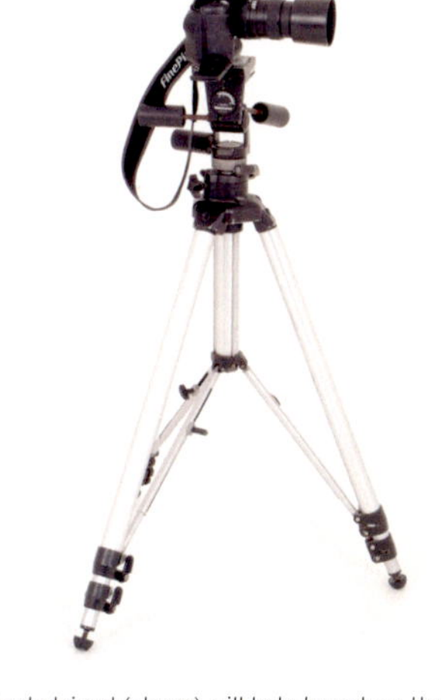

A sturdy tripod (above) will help to reduce the likelihood of camera shake.

Camera shake has spoiled the image (left), by causing image blur. Using a tripod has helped to keep the image on the right sharp, even at a slow shutter speed.

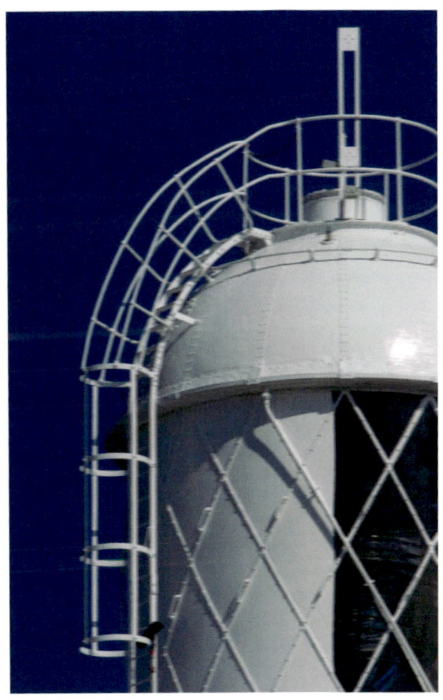

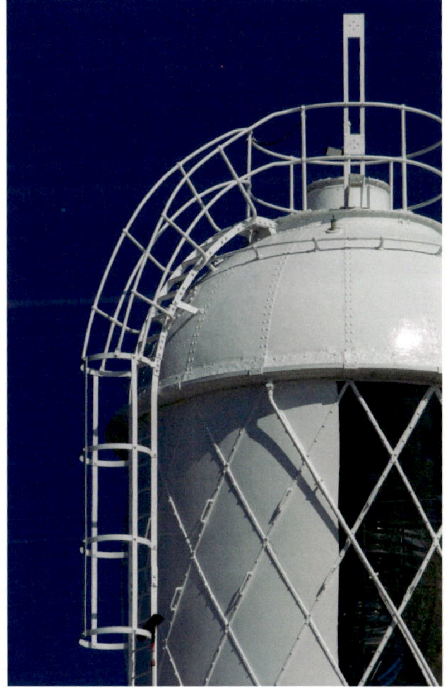

### How do I focus in low light?

Most auto-focus systems in modern cameras operate using a system known as contrast-detection. In low light conditions contrast levels are often too low for AF to work effectively. If the scene you are photographing contains a bright light, such as a streetlight, that is along the same focal plane as your subject, then this can be used as the focus point. Focus can then be locked and the composition reframed, much as if you were focusing on an off-centre subject. This technique can also be applied in Manual Focusing mode.

Another option is to carry with you a very powerful torch, such as the 1m+ candle power torches that are now readily available. The beam from the torch can be shone on the subject and may be bright enough to create enough contrast for AF to operate effectively. A third option is to use intuitive guesswork making use of the focus distance scale on the lens barrel and optimising depth of field.

**Tip**

*Some professional specification cameras have interchangeable viewing screens, enabling the standard screen to be replaced with a special extra-bright screen designed for night photography.*

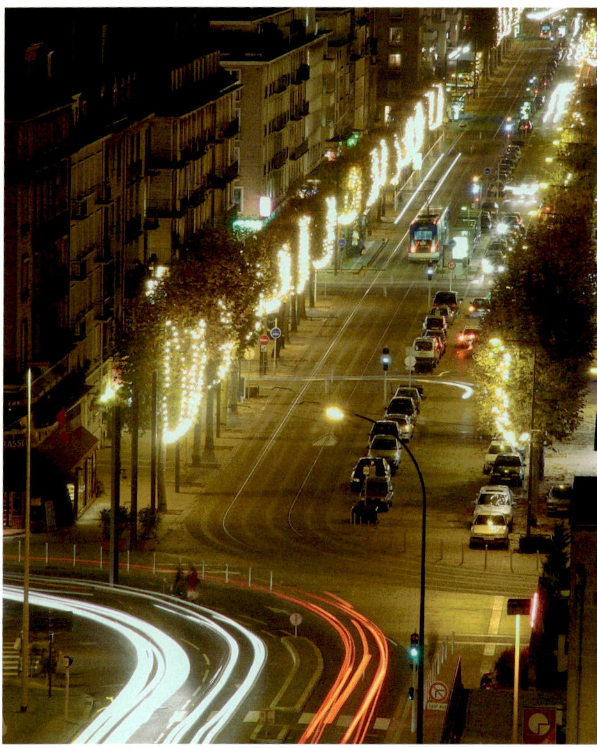

Focusing at night and in low light can be challenging. For this image I used the contrast of the streetlight in the foreground to set my focus point.

### How do I calculate exposure?

One of the most significant problems in calculating exposure in low light conditions is that the level of light may be too low for a light meter to operate effectively. You may also need to overcome the challenges of very high contrast (between the low natural light and any artificial light, for example) and reciprocity failure and digital noise (see pages 74 and 76).

If light levels allow you can use your light meter in the normal way.

If light levels are too low one option is to temporarily increase the ISO rating on the camera to its maximum, assess the EV for the higher ISO and then work backwards to the working ISO based on the law of reciprocity.

For example, if your meter is unable to give an EV at ISO 100, set ISO to 1600 (4 stops more sensitive) and see if that enables the meter to give an EV. If so, take the EV at ISO 1600 and reduce it by 4 stops to calculate the EV at ISO 100.

The following table gives you some examples of how this applies in practice:

| EV @ ISO 1600 | Example exposure | Equivalent EV @ ISO 100 | Equivalent example exposure |
|---|---|---|---|
| 2 | 1 sec at f/2 | -2 | 16 sec at f/2 |
| 3 | $^{1}/_{2}$ sec at f/2 | -1 | 8 sec at f/2 |
| 4 | $^{1}/_{4}$ sec at f/2 | 0 | 4 sec at f/2 |
| 5 | $^{1}/_{8}$ sec at f/2 | 1 | 2 sec at f/2 |
| 6 | $^{1}/_{16}$ sec at f/2 | 2 | 1 sec at f/2 |

One of the best ways to expose in low light situations is from experience using trial and error. This is particularly easy if you have access to a digital camera and can learn 'on the job'. The following table gives some guidelines for exposure in different circumstances, based on my own tests:

| Subject | Recommended exposure at ISO 400 |
|---|---|
| Floodlit building at night - front on | $^{1}/_{4}$ sec at f/4 |
| Floodlit building at night - angled to camera | 1 sec at f/8 |
| Funfairs (freezing motion) | $^{1}/_{125}$ sec at f/2.8 |
| Funfairs (blurring motion) | $^{1}/_{15}$ sec at f/8 |
| Fireworks | Up to 1 min at f/8 |
| Lightning | Several minutes at f/8 |
| Star motion | 4-8 hours at f/8 |
| Moon (on a clear night) | $^{1}/_{500}$ sec at f/11 |
| Floodlit sports events (freeze motion) | $^{1}/_{500}$ sec at f/5.6 |
| Floodlit sports events (blur motion) | $^{1}/_{30}$ sec at f/11 |
| Landscapes (under full moon) | 4 min at f/11 |
| Landscapes (under partial moon) | 8 min at f/11 |
| Street scenes (with pavement lighting) | $^{1}/_{4}$ sec at f/8 |
| Cityscapes (close up) | 2 sec at f/11 |
| Cityscapes (wide angle) | 8 sec at f/11 |

# THE LAW OF RECIPROCITY

## What is the law of reciprocity?

The law of reciprocity relates to exposure and states that any adjustment to one controlling factor (aperture, shutter speed or sensitivity/amplification) must be compensated for by an equal and opposite change in another in order for the same amount of light to reach the film or sensor.

## What is law of reciprocity failure?

The law of reciprocity holds true in digital photography at all times and in film-based photography between certain shutter speeds. However, when either very slow (>1 second) or very fast shutter speeds are used, film's sensitivity to light becomes less even, and the law of reciprocity begins to fail.

## How do I account for reciprocity failure?

When photographing with film at shutter speeds slower than 1 second the film becomes less sensitive to light, which means that the actual exposure needs to be greater than the theoretical exposure based on the law of reciprocity. Most film manufacturers provide tables that indicate the exposure compensation required when using different film types at particular shutter speeds. The table for one of the most popular film brands, Fuji, is reproduced below.

Reciprocity failure is unique to film. The first image (opposite, top) was taken using the basic law of reciprocity to set exposure. However, the very slow shutter speed has resulted in reciprocity failure and under-exposure. By compensating for the reciprocity failure when setting the exposure (opposite, bottom) I have achieved a faithful exposure.

Required exposure compensation for Fuji films

| Film | Shutter speed/Correction filters/Exposure adjustments | | | |
|---|---|---|---|---|
| Fujichrome Velvia for professionals (RVP) | 1/4000 sec. to 1 sec. | 4 sec. | 16 sec. | 64 sec. and longer |
| | None | 5M + 1/3 stop | 10M + 2/3 stop | Not recommended |
| Fujichrome Velvia 100F Professional (RVP100F) | 1/4000 sec. to 1 min. | 2 min. | 4 min. | 8 min. |
| | None | 2.5B + 1/3 stop | 2.5B + 1/2 stop | 2.5B + 2/3 stop |
| Fujichrome Provia 100F Professional (RDPIII) | 1/4000 sec. to 128 sec. | 4 min. | 8min. | |
| | None | 2.5G + 1/3 stop | Not recommended | |
| Fujichrome ASTIA 100 Professional (RAP100F) | 1/4000 sec. to 1 min. | 2 min. | 4 min. | 8 min. |
| | None | 5B + 1/3 stop | 5B + 1/2 stop | 5B + 2/3 stop |
| Fujichrome PROVIA 400F Professional (RHPIII) | 1/4000 sec. to 32 sec. | 64 sec. | 2 min. to 4 min. | 8 min. |
| | None | 5G + 2/3 stop | 7.5G + 1 stop | Not recommended |
| Fujichrome 64T Type II Professional (RTPII) | 1/4000 sec. to 1/30 sec. | 1/15 sec. to 64 sec | 2 min. | 4 min. |
| | Not recommended | None | None + 1/3 stop | None + 1/2 stop |
| Fujichrome Sensia 100 (RA) | 1/4000 sec. to 1 min. | 2 min. | 4 min. | 8 min. |
| | None | 5B + 1/3 stop | 5B + 1/2 stop | 5B + 2/3 stop |
| Fujichrome Sensia 200 (RM) | 1/4000 sec. to 32 sec. | 64 sec. | 2 min. to 4 min. | 8 min. |
| | None | 5G + 2/3 stop | 7.5G + 1 stop | Not recommended |
| Fujichrome Sensia 400 (RH) | 1/4000 sec. to 32 sec. | 64 sec. | 2 min. to 4 min. | 8 min. |
| | None | 5G + 2/3 stop | 7.5G + 1 stop | Not recommended |

So, for example, if you were photographing with Fuji Velvia slide film and were using a shutter speed of 4 seconds, you would need to increase the metered exposure by 1/3 stop in order to compensate for reciprocity failure.

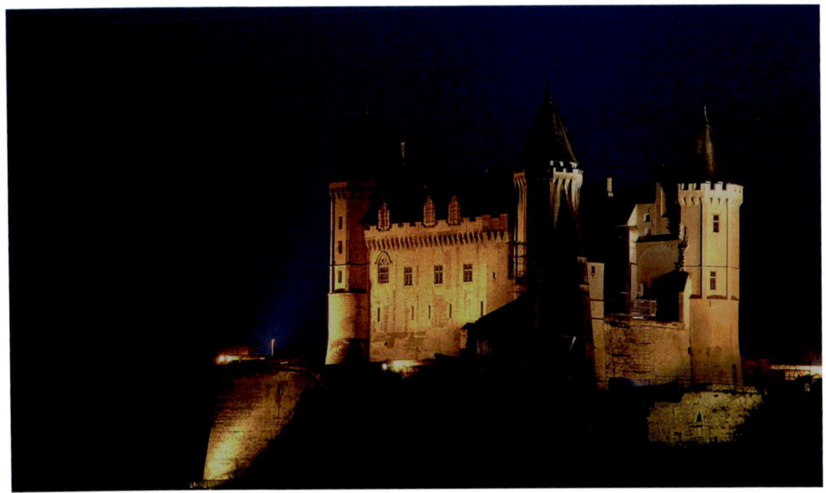

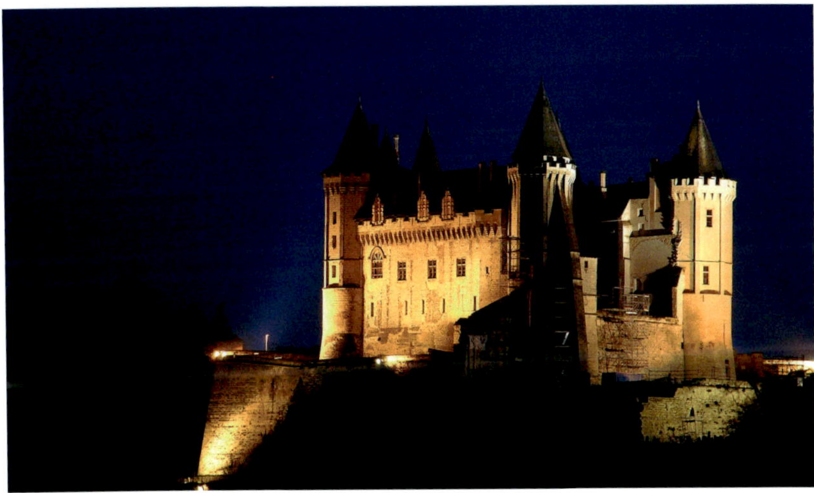

**See also**

*Digital noise (page 76)*

**Does law of reciprocity failure apply in digital photography?**

No. Law of reciprocity failure is specific to film. However, long time exposures in digital photography cause a digital-specific phenomenon referred to as noise.

# DIGITAL NOISE

## What is digital noise?

Digital noise appears on digital files as random, unrelated pixels, often of bright colours. Noise is often prevalent in shadow areas and degrades image quality, as can be seen in the comparative images, shown opposite.

A high ISO rating (ISO 1600) has resulted in digital noise affecting particularly the shadow areas in the image of a lioness photographed at night.

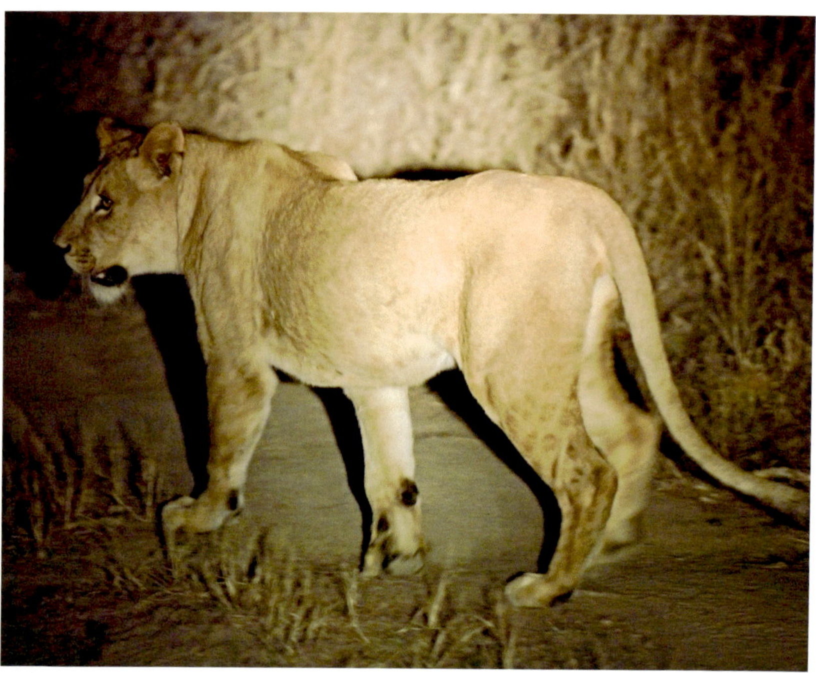

## What causes digital noise?

Digital noise is caused by the heat generated by the sensor, which is particularly noticeable during long time exposures as the sensor gets hotter the longer it is charged; and by the process of amplification used to increase the light signal at higher ISO ratings.

## How do I overcome digital noise?

The easiest way to avoid digital noise is to use only low ISO ratings (less than ISO 400) and to maintain shutter speeds faster than 1 second. Failing this option most DSLR cameras have a noise reduction (NR) function in the menu options and this can be enabled whenever ISO exceeds 400 or shutter speeds drop below 1 second. In some cases the NR function will completely eradicate visible noise, sometimes it will only reduce it.

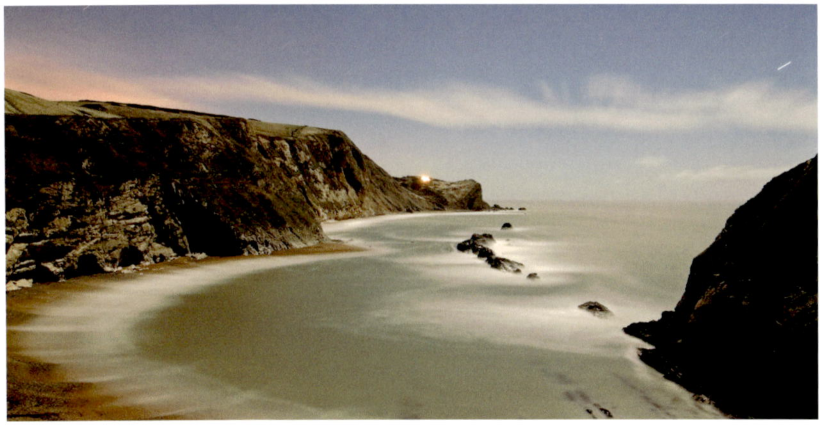

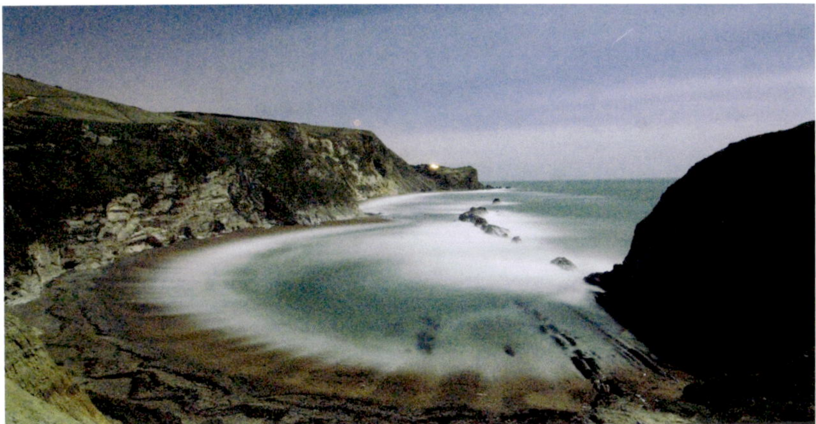

## Can I deal with digital noise at the processing stage?

In a limited way digital noise can be removed using image-processing software, such as Adobe Photoshop. However, be aware that any such retouching will always result in a compromise elsewhere in the image. When removing digital noise the compromise is typically with image edge sharpness.

Digital noise is a particular problem when using a digital camera for night and low light photography. Many DSLR cameras have a noise reduction function that helps to reduce the effect of noise.

# COPING WITH HIGH-CONTRAST SCENES

## Why is high contrast a problem?

All film and digital sensors have a limited ability to record detail in shadows and highlights simultaneously. Film has limited latitude and digital sensors have limited dynamic range. If the brightness range in the scene exceeds the latitude of the film or dynamic range of the sensor then detail will be lost in either the shadow areas or the highlights, or possibly both - see the diagram below.

In bright conditions, it's very likely that the subject brightness range will extend beyond the capability of the film/sensor to record detail in both shadows and highlights simultaneously.

Latitude (dynamic range) and subject brightness range

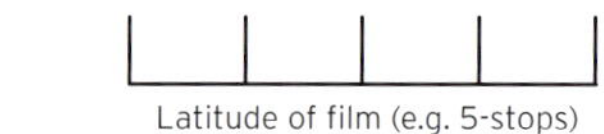

Latitude of film (e.g. 5-stops)

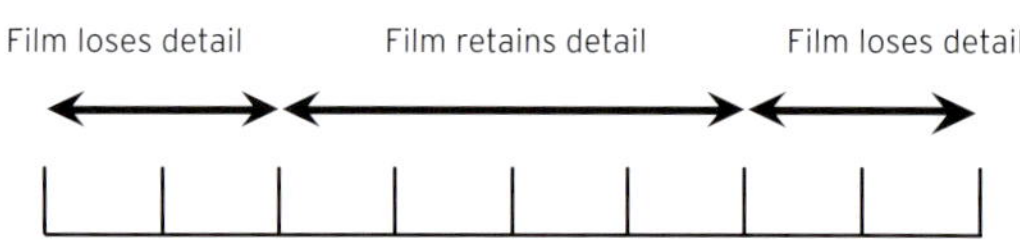


Subject brightness range (e.g. 9-stops)

## How do you calculate the subject brightness range?

First take a meter reading of the brightest part of the scene and then calculate the exposure for the darkest part of the scene. Work out the difference between the two exposures in stops and this gives you your SBR. If the SBR is greater than the latitude of the film being used (or the dynamic range of the sensor) then the camera will be unable to record detail in all areas of the scene. Unless the brighter area of the scene is of a uniform shape it is unlikely that you'll be able to use a NDG filter to even the tones. If this is the case you must compromise and expose either for the highlights or for the shadows, sacrificing detail in the brightest or darkest tones, depending on your decision.

## Is it better to expose for the shadows or the highlights?

Typically it is better to expose for the highlights, retaining detail in the whites. This is especially so in digital photography due to the nature in which sensors record light information. There is also a psychological reason: humans are used to seeing areas of dense shadow in everyday life and so they don't look out of place in a photograph. The opposite isn't true of burned-out highlights.

In the first image (opposite, top) the camera has failed to cope with the high level of contrast in this scene and the highlights have blown out. By exposing for the highlights detail has been retained in the white water (opposite, bottom).

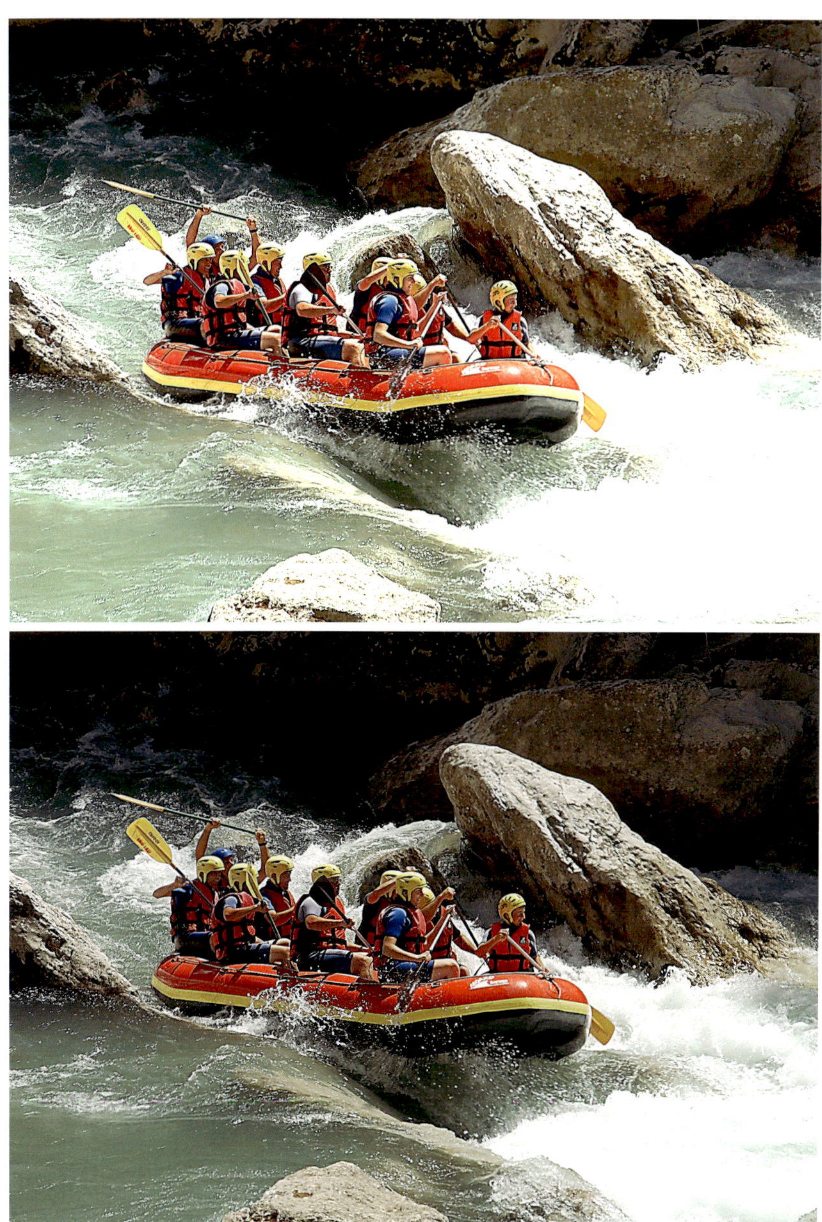

# WORKING UNDER MOONLIGHT

## How does moonlight differ from sunlight?

Moonlight is simply sunlight reflected off the surface of the moon. As such, you might expect it to have the same qualities as sunlight. However, the intensity of moonlight is much reduced, compared to sunlight. In this sense, although non-diffused moonlight is directional, it has a quality similar to that of bounced light, being softer. One of the nice things about photographing under moonlight is that you get the benefits of directional lighting, for example, form-giving shadows, with the soft quality of omni-directional light.

### Tip

*A good website for calculating moonlight exposures is: http://mkaz.com/photo/tools/expcalc.html*

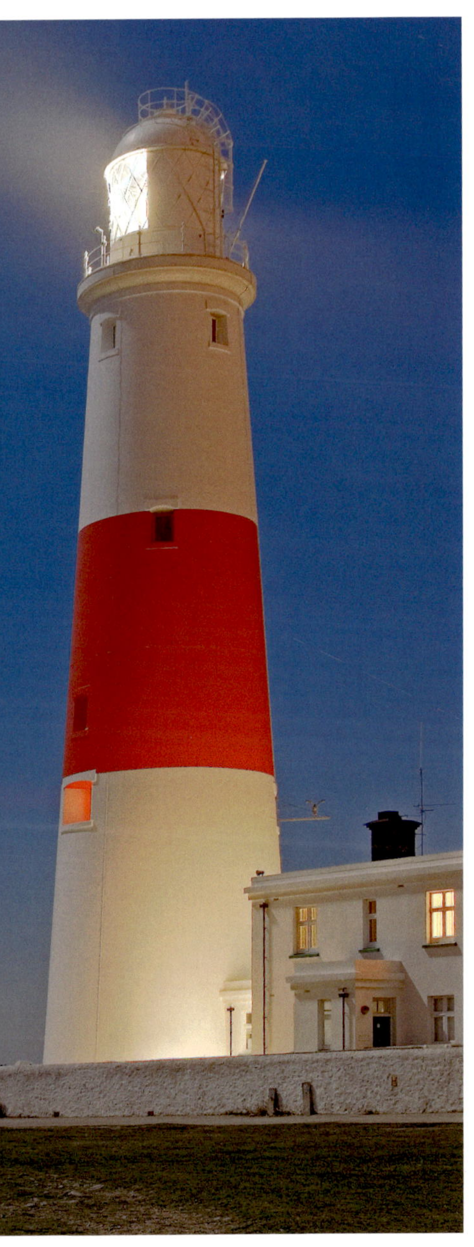

### How do I calculate exposure for moonlight photography?

Light from the moon is around 18 stops dimmer than direct sunlight. Using this as a guideline it is possible to employ the Sunny-F16 rule in relation to photography using full moonlight on a clear night. For example, the Sunny-F16 rule states that the exposure, using an ISO 100 film (or digital equivalent), would be 1/100 at f/16. To calculate the equivalent exposure for moonlight, simply reduce this exposure by 18 stops giving an exposure of 24 minutes at f/16 (or 12 minutes at f/11 or 6 minutes at f/8), without accounting for reciprocity law failure.

For exposures under less than full-moon conditions, use the following guide to exposure compensation:

| Moon phase | Exposure compensation |
|---|---|
| Gibbous moon | +1.5 stops |
| Quarter moon | +3.5 stops |
| Crescent moon | +6.5 stops |
| New moon | Impractical |

### What is the colour temperature of moonlight?

As moonlight is simply reflected sunlight the colour temperature is roughly the same as normal daylight (around 5,500K).

The soft quality of light from the moon has helped to give this image an ethereal quality.

SECTION FIVE

# CLOSE-UP AND MACRO PHOTOGRAPHY

Great lighting plays an essential part in creating outstanding images of the natural world, revealing all of its tiny details and intricate beauty. But lighting for close-up photography also provides many new challenges. What is the right type of light source? Where do you position the light source? How do you take account of the effect of magnification factor on exposure? The following section provides answers to all of these questions.



Macro photography provides a whole new world of lighting challenges.

# MACRO PHOTOGRAPHY IN NATURAL LIGHT

**What is the ideal lighting for macro photography?**

Many expert macro photographers like to work with soft lighting from a diffused source due to its reduced levels of contrast, which helps to maintain detail in areas of shadow and highlight simultaneously.

**See also**

*Quality of light (page 24)*

Macro photography opens up a whole new world of creative possibilities for the photographer.

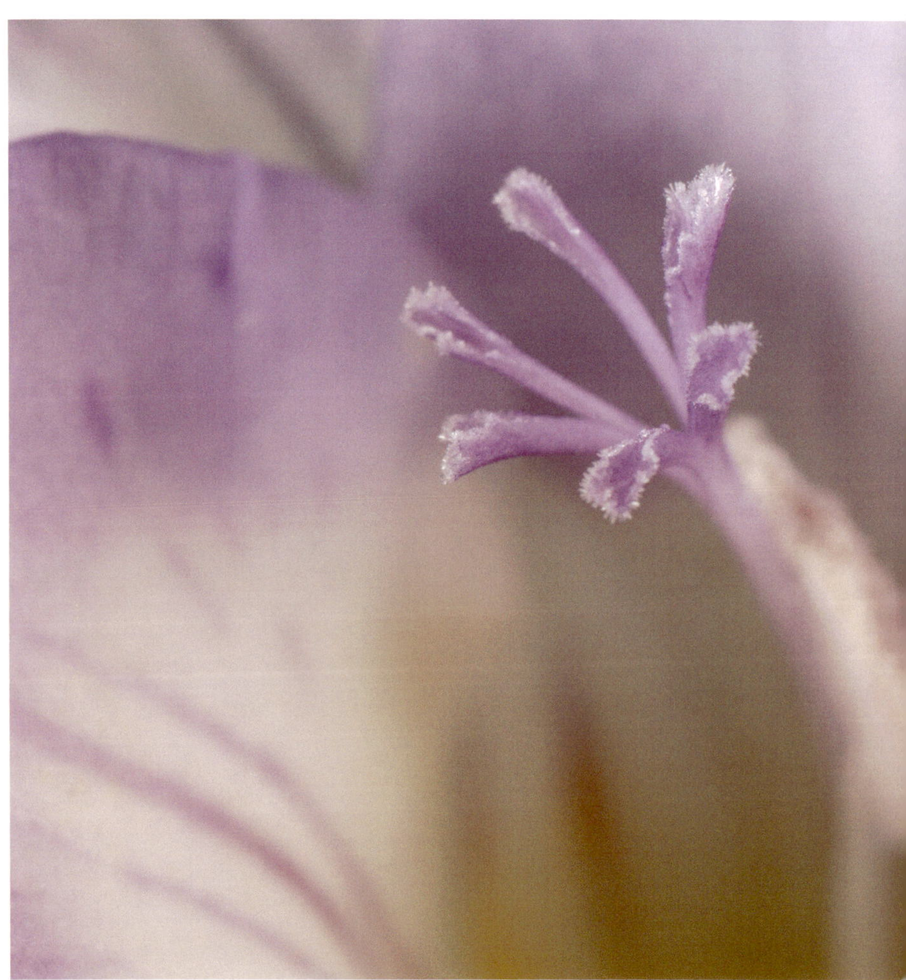

**See also**

*The time of day (page 52)*

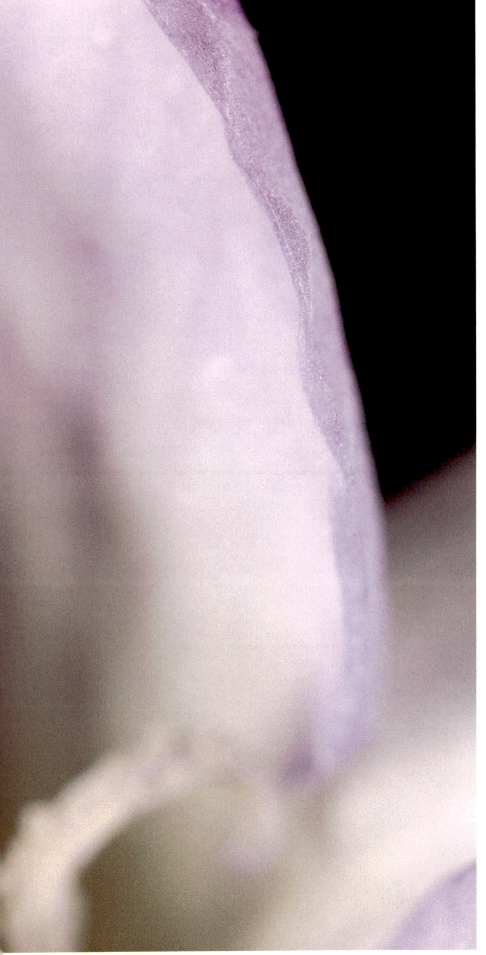

### When is the best time of day for macro photography outdoors?

Because side lighting helps to accentuate texture and form, early to mid-morning or late afternoon are often the ideal times for macro photography outdoors. Beware, however, of lighting at this time that is too direct, as this will cause excessive shadows and increase tonal range beyond the capabilities of the film or sensor.

### Can I change lighting conditions outdoors?

Because of the small size of the subject it is eminently possible to alter lighting conditions specific to your subject. For example, a diffuser held in place between the sun and the subject will change hard direct light to soft omni-directional light.

Conversely, if you want direct light on a cloudy day, cut a hole in a piece of card and position the card above the subject. The hole will act to funnel omni-directional light through a single source.

In using either technique you will need to be aware of light loss, particularly if metering with a hand-held meter.

Reflectors can also be used to help illuminate shadow areas, either with direct or omni-directional lighting, by placing the reflector on the opposite side of the main light source facing towards the subject.

**See also**

*Panel reflectors and diffusers (page 49)*

# USING FLASH IN MACRO PHOTOGRAPHY

Special flash units (macroflash) are available for macro and close-up photography (right).

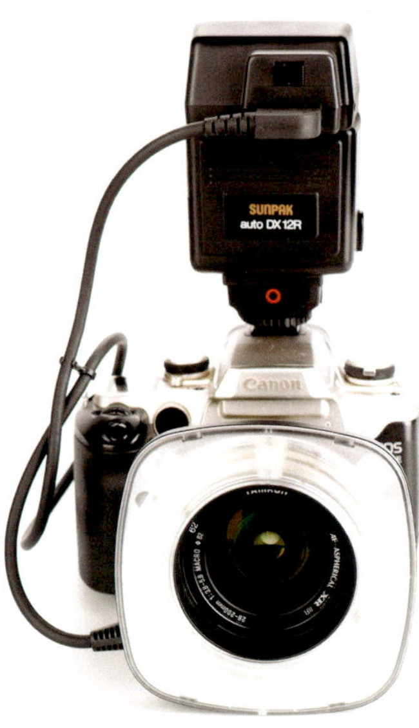


A macroflash unit, specially designed for use in close-up photography.

## What is the ideal flash unit?

The problem with most external flash units is they are simply too powerful to be used so close to the subject, even when they are set to reduced power output levels. The small built-in flash units on many modern cameras are small enough, however they are badly positioned, being head-on to the subject.

The ideal type of flash unit used in close-up photography is a specialist macroflash unit, which is designed specifically for macro and close-up work. Alternatively, a small, less powerful flash (guide number of around 15 at ISO 100) positioned off-camera would be suitable for most macro applications.

**See also**

*Filters for managing contrast (page 46)*

## What is macroflash?

Macroflash units are specially designed for close-up photography. Typically they consist of a ring-like unit housing two flash tubes, which fits around and attaches to the lens barrel. Advanced units enable independent control of the two flash tubes, enabling the photographer to adjust power output of either or both.

This makes it possible to create a compositionally stronger image using mixed light levels. When using less sophisticated units it's possible to achieve the same effect by placing a neutral density filter over one side of the macroflash.

In more recent years, some manufacturers have produced macroflash units with remote, independently positioned multiple units, which has added to their flexibility.

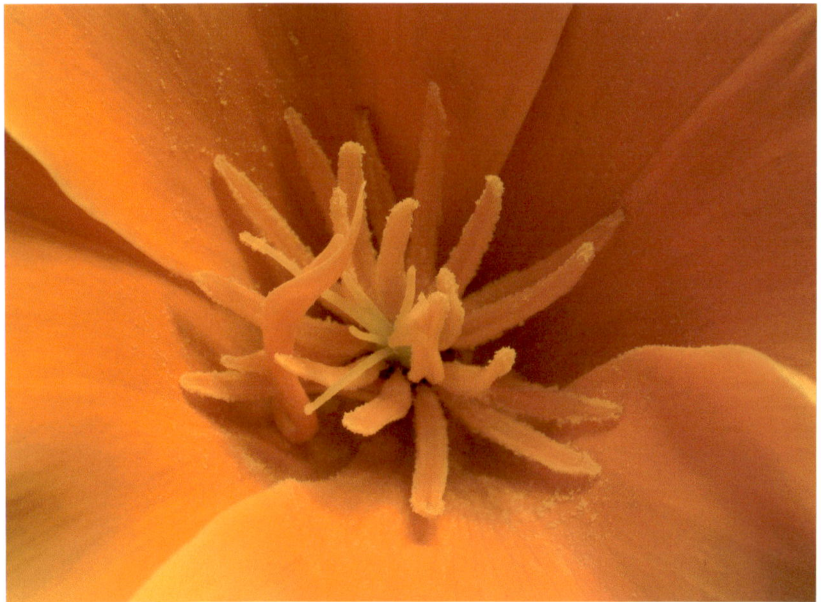

## Is a twin-flash set-up the same thing as macroflash?

Twin-flash set-ups that use two independent flash units attached close to the camera via brackets effectively achieve the same result as macroflash, in that they provide uniform lighting. The disadvantage of this set-up is the possible occurrence of double shadows. This can be overcome by adjusting the power output of one of the units (or moving it further away from the subject).

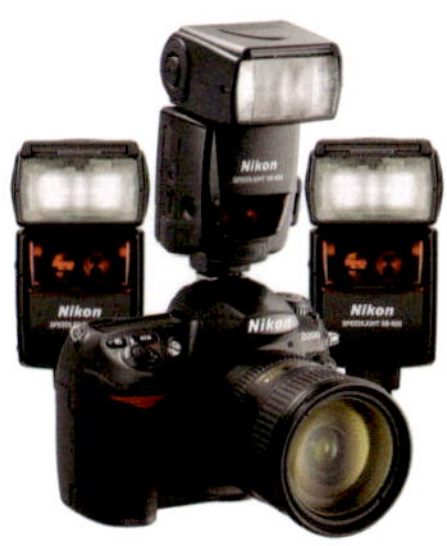

## What if I've got only a single flash unit?

You can still manage good macro images with a single flash, if the flash is used effectively. One option is to use the flash in conjunction with a small reflector, placed directly opposite the flash, which will act as a secondary source of illumination. The advantage of this set-up is that the secondary light source can never be more powerful than the prime source, which improves the tonal quality of the scene. You also avoid the phenomenon of twin highlights when photographing insects and similar creatures.

**See also**

*Avoiding common problems (page 92)*

Modern flash systems are highly sophisticated and enable simple implementation of multiple-flash set-ups.

### What is the best positioning for the flash unit?

Ideally single and multiple flash units (non macroflash) should be positioned at an angle of around 45 degrees to the subject, and slightly above the subject. This will mimic daylight around the time of mid-morning and late afternoon. The acute nature of this angle of light will cause tiny shadows to form, accentuating detail and texture and adding to the overall impression of sharpness.

**Tip**

*When working with non-automated flash for close-up photography it is often a sensible idea to bracket your images, taking several identical shots at 0.5 to 1 stop over- and under-exposed from your calculated exposure.*

### What are the advantages of modern automated flash units?

The level of sophistication of modern dedicated, automated flash units makes them more intuitive to the subject. By working in conjunction with data from the camera, such as focus distance, they are able to produce far more accurate results than ever before, even for close-up work.

Working in conjunction with the camera's built-in exposure meter also reduces the need for lengthy exposure calculations to take into account magnification factor and other light-reducing factors that come into play during macro photography.

The flash unit should be positioned to give the best direction of light relevant to the subject being photographed, as in the image below.

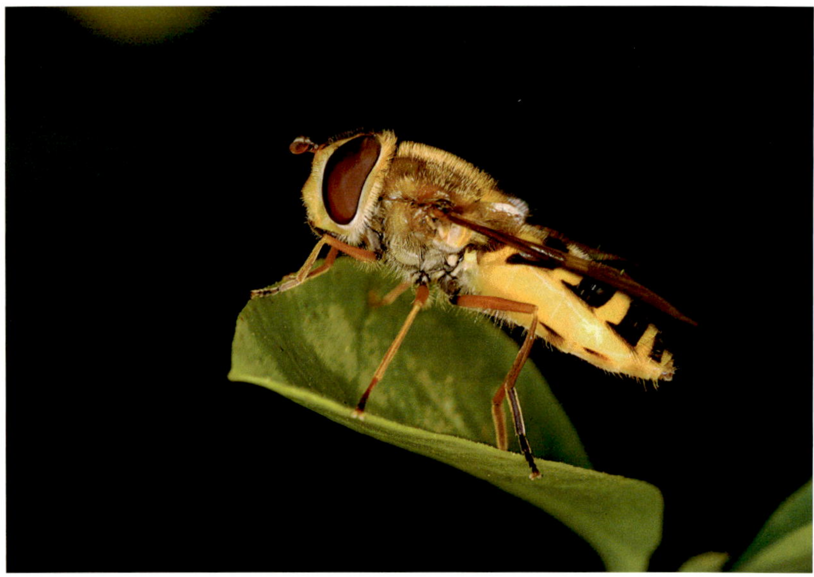

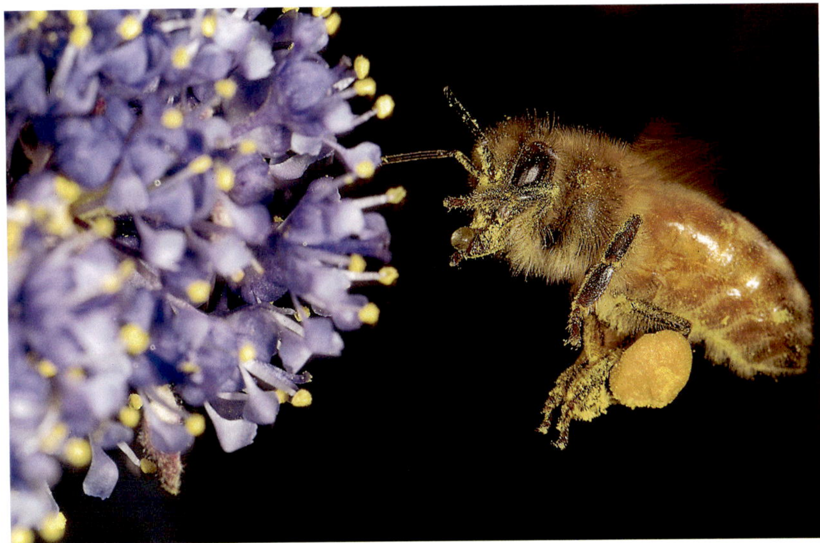

The use of flash can help to capture startling images of even the most challenging of subjects.

## Can I use non-automated flash?

Of course, it's still possible to use non-automated flash. After all, what did we do before all this technology came along to help us? Often the use of non-automated units involves a lot of testing of flash position before using the flash in a live environment. The following test will help you to understand the distance from which your non-automated flash operates best.

## How do I test flash-to-subject distance?

**Step 1** Set the camera on a tripod with the flash unit attached off-camera at an angle of 45 degrees to the subject. Make a note of the flash-to-subject distance.

**Step 2** Take a series of test images at different lens apertures (e.g. f/5.6, f/8, f/11, f/16, etc.) keeping the camera in a fixed position.

**Step 3** Examine the images. If they are all too bright, move the flash further from the subject and repeat the test. Similarly, if all the images are dark, move the flash closer. Maintain the same angle of flash (45 degrees).

**Step 4** By this trial-and-error method, identify the best exposure at f/16 and make a note of the flash-to-subject distance. This will form your standard shooting position (angle and distance) when using non-automated flash.

### Tip

*When photographing very bright or very dark subjects and calculating exposure manually, allow around -1 stop exposure compensation for very bright subjects and between +0.5 to 1 stop for dark subjects.*

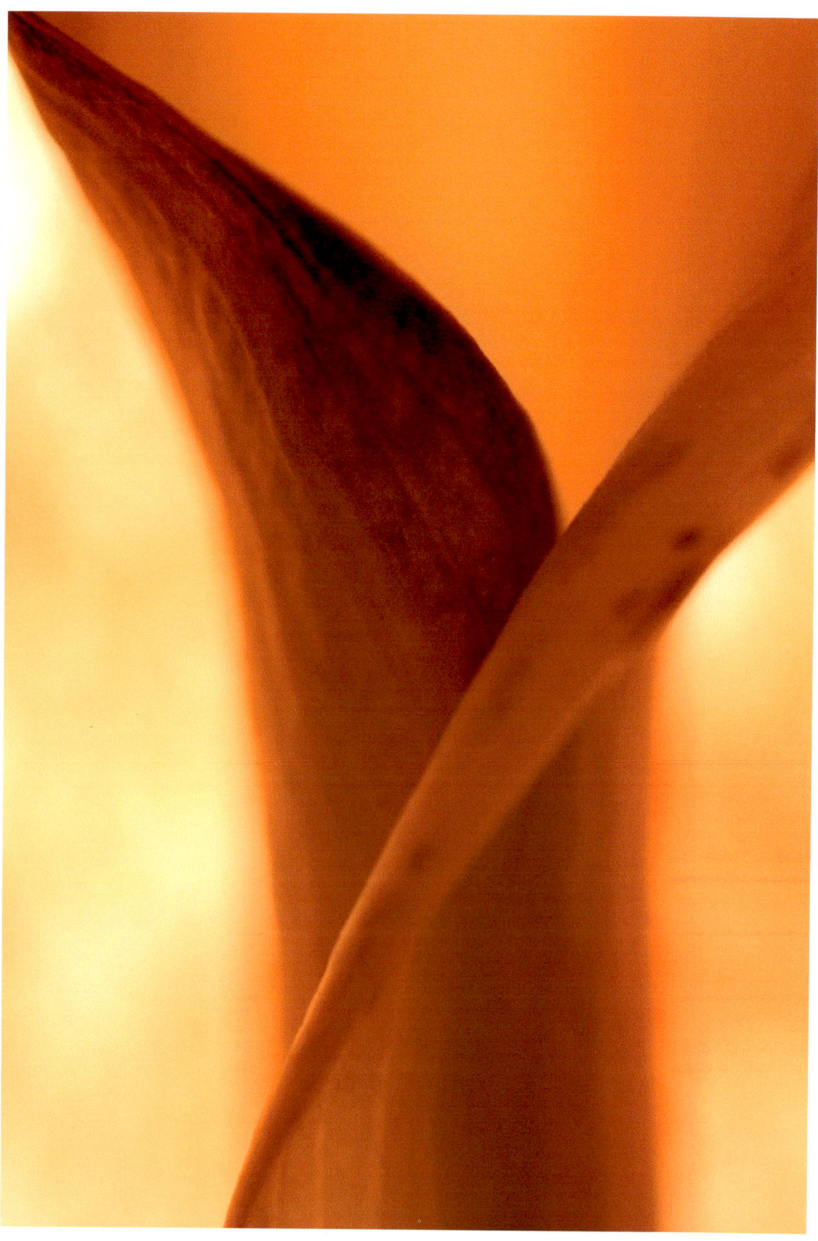

### What is continuous-source artificial light?

Continuous-source artificial light is simply light from a constant source, such as a tungsten bulb or halogen light, rather than from an instant-on/instant-off flash.

### When would I use continuous-source lighting?

Continuous-source artificial lighting is more likely to be used in a studio environment rather than in the field, where it is less practical. For example, it's possible to set up a permanent close-up shooting table for studio macro work, where the light is provided via something like angle-poise lamps.

### Are there advantages to using continuous-source artificial lighting?

The main advantage to this type of lighting is that it's possible to immediately see the effects of the lighting on the subject, which is not the case with flash (without the aid of a digital camera with an instant replay facility).

The low power of some forms of continuous-source artificial light is also better suited to close-up work and the lighting can be used with diffusers and reflectors just as easily as can flash units. However, one potential problem is the heat they give off, which can be deadly to some small creatures.

Continuous-source lighting enables the photographer to see the effects of the lighting set-up prior to recording the image - useful when shooting with film when instant digital review is unavailable.

#### Tip

*When using tungsten or fluorescent lighting remember to compensate for the difference in colour temperature using optical filters or the WB setting on the camera.*

### Are all continuous-source lights suitable for macro photography?

On the whole, yes, so long as colour temperature is correctly balanced using the White Balance control on the camera (e.g. fluorescent for fluorescent lighting and incandescent for tungsten lighting). However, some tungsten lights can run very hot and, when placed close to a living subject, such as an insect, the heat from the lamp can literally cook the creature. When working at very close distances, fluorescent lighting is a cool running continuous source of light, which is far safer to work with.

#### See also

*Colour temperature (page 17)*

## How do I avoid black backgrounds?

One of the potential hazards in using flash, particularly low-power flash, is light fall-off, which can result in the occurrence of black backgrounds. Black backgrounds are not necessarily a bad thing. For example, they can help to isolate a subject by eliminating distractions. However, many photographers argue that they look unnatural and prefer to avoid them.

A simple solution is to place a naturally coloured piece of material (e.g. a T-shirt, cloth or card) behind the subject at a distance far enough to avoid it being within the zone of sharpness but close enough to fill the frame and to fall within the range of the flash.

Light fall-off results in the background being under-exposed to such an extent that it appears featureless black.

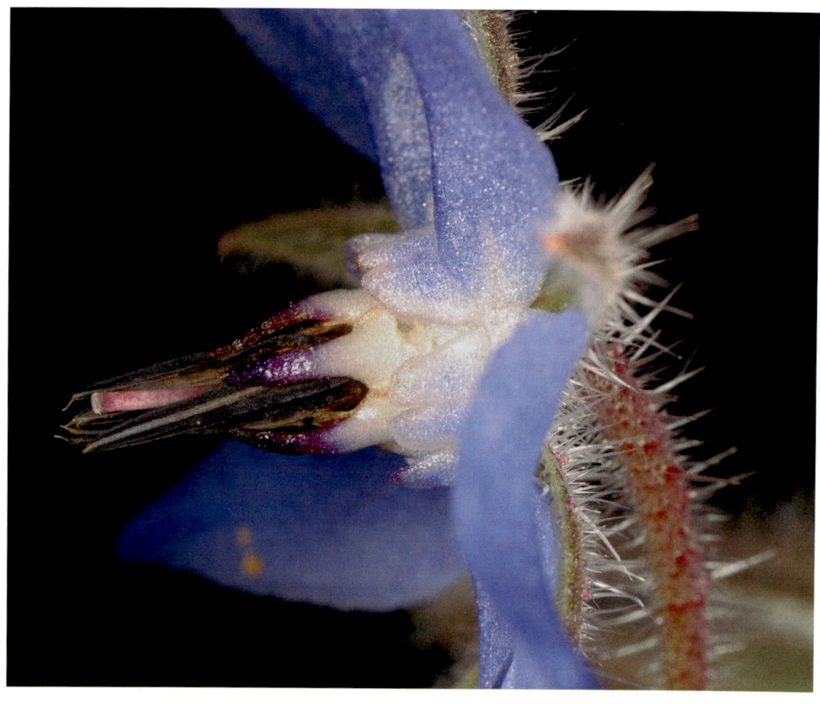

**Tip**

*Artificial backgrounds can be quickly assembled using a small framework, some clips and a piece of naturally coloured (i.e. green, brown, tan etc.) cloth.*

### How do I avoid distracting backgrounds?

Outdoors backgrounds can get distracting, particularly when strong colours are visible - even if they are blurred. Try minor changes of camera angle, to the side and up and down, to see if this will provide a cleaner background. Also, shooting at wider apertures will decrease depth of field and increase the amount of blur, which may be enough to diffuse detail.

Placing a natural-looking backdrop closer to the subject, enabling some light from the flash to illuminate it, overcomes the occurrence of black backgrounds.

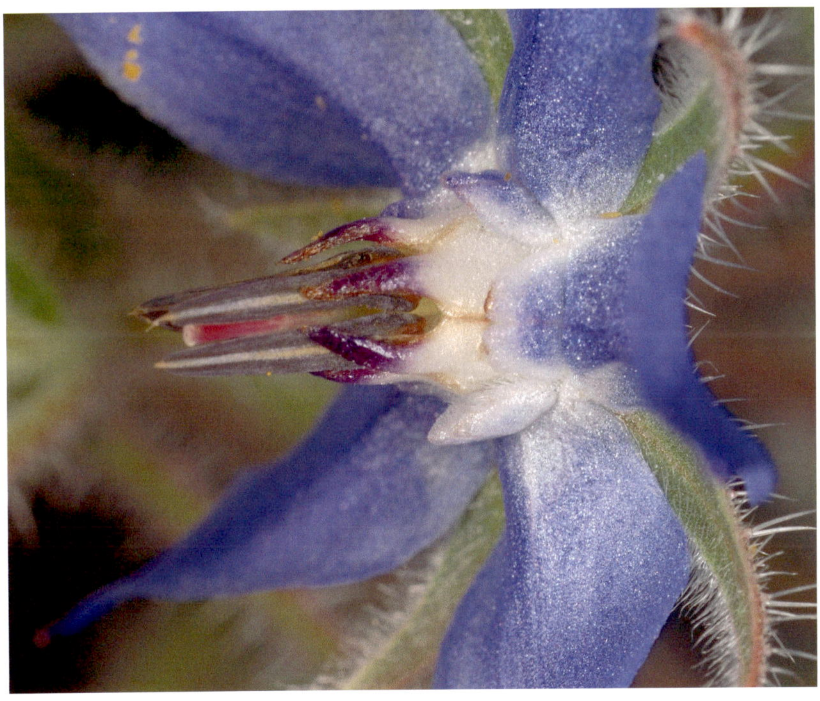

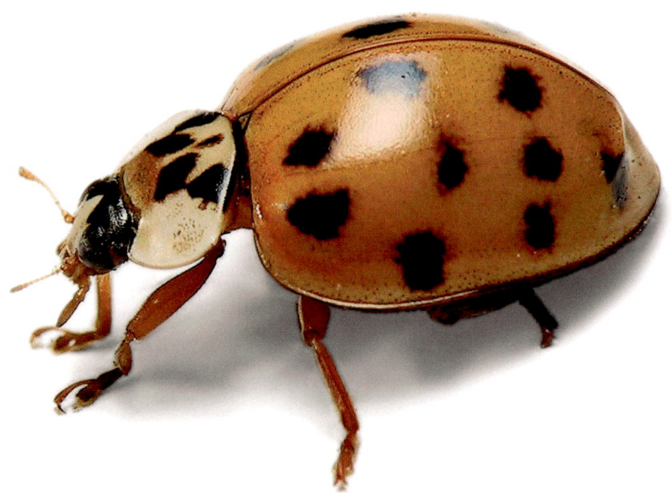

The shiny surface of some subjects, such as this ladybird, can cause hotspots to occur when flash is used.

### How do I cope with highly reflective surfaces?

The highly reflective surfaces of some subjects, such as beetles, can cause hot spots to occur when flash is used. A simple solution to avoiding hot spots is to use a diffuser over the flash head to soften the quality of the light.

**See also**

*Panel reflectors and diffusers (page 49)*

**Tip**

*One method for ensuring single catchlights is to use a single flash unit in conjunction with an appropriately placed reflector (positioned opposite the flash unit, directing light back on to the subject). The reflector will throw light back into the shadow areas to lift them. For more information on using reflectors, see page 49.*

### What are twin highlights and how do I avoid them?

When light catches an animal's or insect's eyes a catchlight is produced. When using two flash units simultaneously it's likely that twin catchlights (highlights) will occur. This will look unnatural because we never see twin highlights in the natural world (the earth having only one sun).

There is little that can be done at the point of capture to avoid twin highlights, other than using a single flash unit. However, the offending second catchlight can always be cloned out using image-processing software, such as Adobe Photoshop, during any digital processing stage.

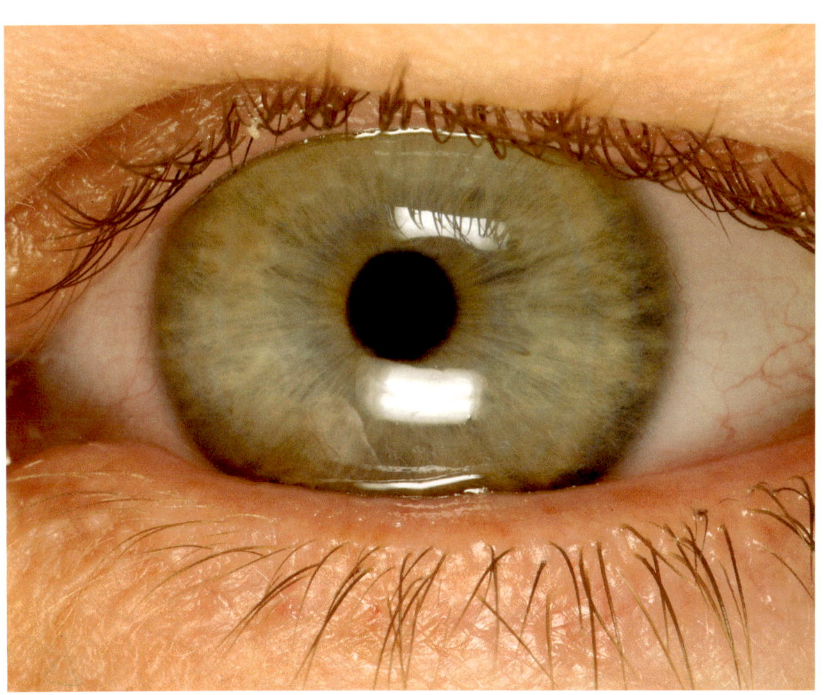

Using multiple flash units may cause twin highlights to appear in eyes, which look unnatural because we have only one sun and therefore expect to see single catchlights.

SECTION SIX

# THE DAYLIGHT STUDIO

When photographing indoors the natural instinct is to reach for flash. However, there's another option - the daylight studio. A well-lit room and a few inexpensive accessories can make an excellent alternative to an expensive studio set-up. But how do you go about creating a daylight studio and getting the most from the available light? The following section details the necessities of shooting indoors with sunlight.



A daylight studio can offer a wealth of opportunities when photographing indoors.

# SETTING UP A DAYLIGHT STUDIO

**How do I choose the best room for a daylight studio?**

There are three important factors when considering a room in your home as a daylight studio. First of all it needs to be large enough to provide room for you and your camera, the model and any props and backgrounds that you might use. Ideally you'd want at least 3 metres (10 feet) between you and the model and a further 1.5-2 metres (4-6 feet) between the model and the background. All in all, ideally you'd want a minimum of 6 metres (20 feet) of linear space.

Secondly, the room needs to be well lit. A large window or doorway will provide enough light and also an element of flexibility. Better still is a room with two or more light points, such as two windows, a window and outside door, or a window and a skylight. The larger the light source the more flexibility you will have with possible lighting set-ups.

Finally you need to consider anyone else who will have or want to have access to the room, such as other family members. This is particularly important if you are working with a model, as constant interruptions will not only adversely affect your workflow but will leave the model frustrated, which ultimately will show in the images.

**How do I turn a living room into a studio?**

First of all you will need to clear the room to make space for you, your equipment and the subject. The floor should always be kept free of clutter and make sure there is a natural walkway around immovable objects.

Using the light source as a guide, consider the areas of the room suitable for posing your model or positioning the subject. Look through the viewfinder of your camera and check the background. Keep an eye open for distracting and obtrusive elements that will detract from your image.

Anything that isn't a part of your composition and may overlap the picture frame, such as pictures on the wall, vases and knick-knacks, should be moved well out of sight.

**Can I use a living room without moving all the furniture?**

Some rooms lend themselves to studio photography with models. An obvious example is using a bedroom for glamour-type shots, or even a bathroom. However, you will need to ensure that any room you use is large enough to give you and the model some space to work in, is clean and uncluttered, and has sufficient light for photography.

# USEFUL EQUIPMENT FOR A DAYLIGHT STUDIO

## How do I set up a daylight studio?

You will need a form of seating for the model, which should be positioned relative to the light source or sources. A background can be either a plainly painted wall, a single-tone bed sheet, or similar, hung from the ceiling, or a purpose-bought background set, consisting of a stand, holder and paper roll.

A translucent sheet can be used as a diffuser when covering the window or doorway, which will give you flexibility in the quality of light you have to work with. A coloured, translucent sheet will affect the colour of the light entering through the opening. For example, an orange sheet will give the light a warm cast. Be careful not to overdo this effect, as a pleasant cast can quickly turn into a lurid overtone.

You may also want to add a reflector to your collection, to help lighten areas of shadow. A few props will also provide more options for picture ideas.

**See also**

*Panel reflectors and diffusers (page 49)*

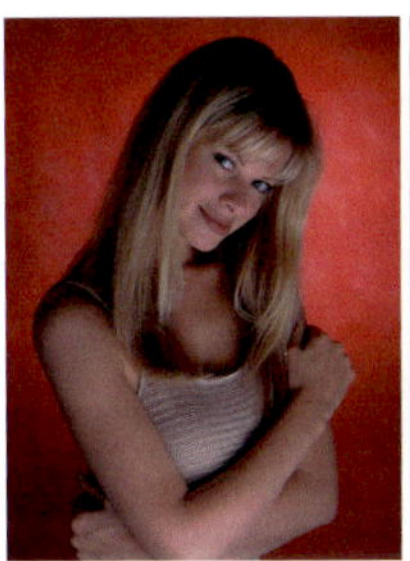
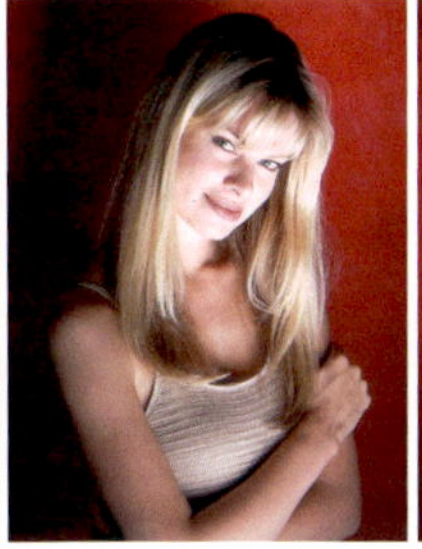
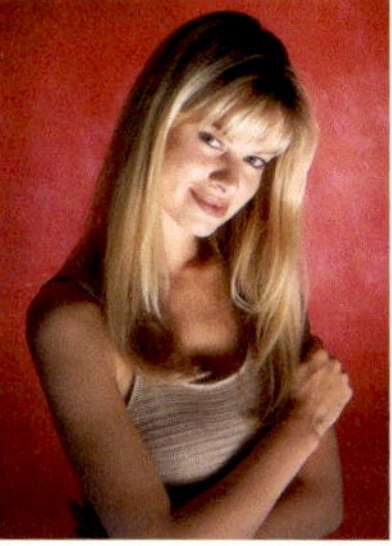
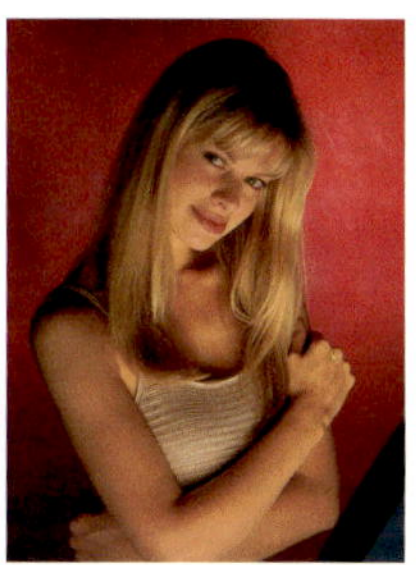

A range of accessories are available for use in a studio environment. This set of four images shows how different-coloured reflectors alter the appearance of an image.

## Do I need to spend a fortune on expensive gear?

There's no doubt you could spend a fortune on expensive gear, but there really is no need to. Most of the props you might want to use can be found around the house, as can seating for the model. A kitchen stool will often suffice.

The background can be simply a plain coloured wall or a sheet draped over a suitable frame or hung from the ceiling. Similarly, a bed sheet will act as a diffuser and a reflector can be simply a piece of white, silver or gold card.

# SOURCES OF LIGHT

### What are the main available sources of light for a daylight studio?

There are three possible natural light sources in a daylight studio. The most obvious is a window but a doorway leading outside, French windows and even a skylight are all possible sources of light. Ideally a room would have two or more sources that can be opened or blacked out, as required.

### Can I change the direction of light?

You can't change the direction of light from the source but you can achieve the same thing by moving the model or subject relative to the source. For example, at 90 degrees to a window a model will be side lit. Turn him or her 90 degrees in one or other direction and you will have either backlighting (for silhouettes and rim lighting) or front lighting.

**See also**

*Direction of light (page 28)*

Sources of light

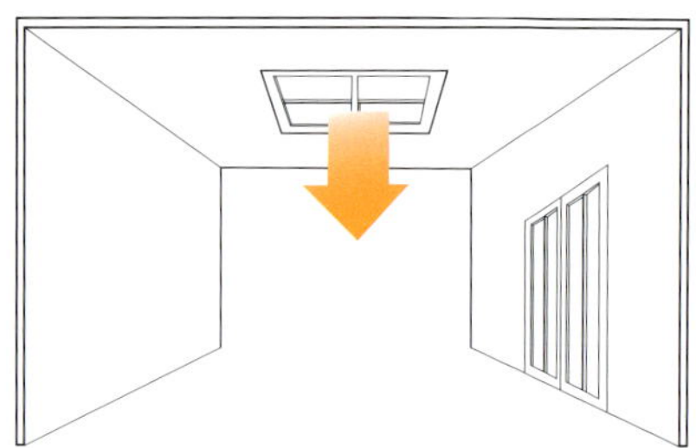

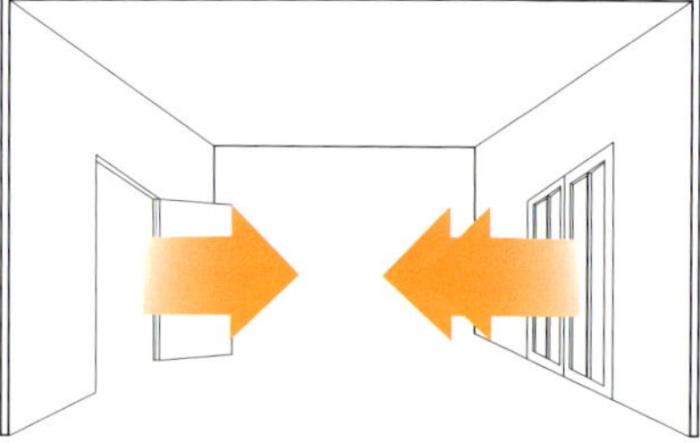

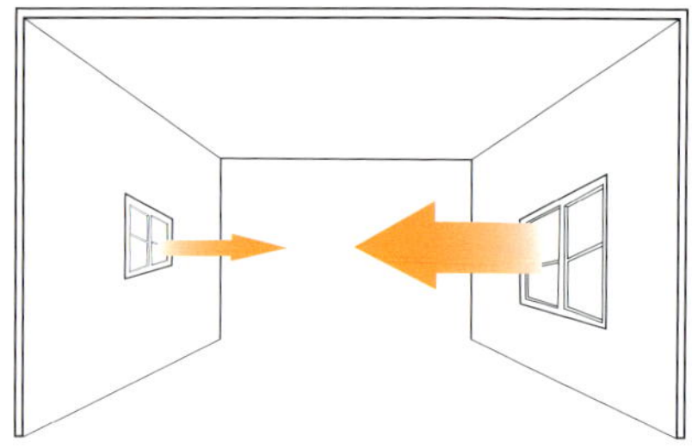

Windows, doors and even skylights are all sources of light in a daylight studio.

### What are the differences between light sources?

Doorways and windows will typically provide side lighting, while a skylight will give overhead lighting. Generally the former is more flexible and provides better light for photography. Windows are also often better-placed and more practical to work with. However, patio doors can be a large source of light. Lighting from a skylight has a similar quality to natural light outdoors around noon.

**See also**

*Direction of light (page 28)*

**See also**

*Quality of light (page 24)*

## Can I alter the size of the light source and quality of light?

Changing the size of the source will affect the quality of light. For example, hard lighting can be changed to soft lighting by adding a diffuser to scatter the light. And soft lighting from a large source can be made hard by reducing the size of the light source, for example by blacking out all but a small area of a window.

A small window may provide a direct light source but can be easily modified with a form of diffuser to create soft, omni-directional lighting.

Size of light source

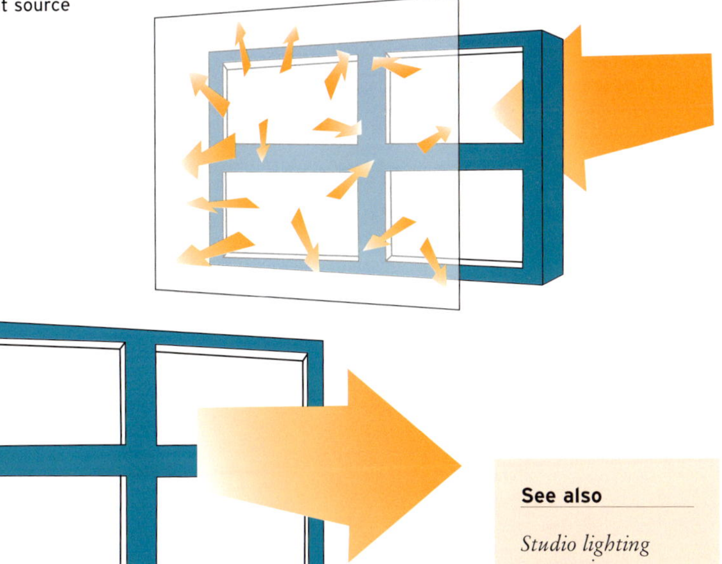

**See also**

*Studio lighting accessories (page 134)*

**Tip**

*Your own home isn't the only possibility for a daylight studio. Other buildings, such as barns, can make ideal spaces for a studio, or you can hire a professional studio.*

## Can I change the colour of light?

By placing a form of coloured filter between the light source and your model or subject, you can create a similar effect to using a coloured gel over a studio flash head. Coloured lighting can be used to create interesting lighting effects but should not be overdone.

# USING FILL-IN FLASH IN A DAYLIGHT STUDIO

### When would I use fill-in flash?

The principle behind using fill-in flash in the studio is no different to when using it outdoors. Its purpose is to add illumination into areas of shadow and reduce levels of contrast. In this way, it can be used in place of a reflector.

### Where should I position the flash?

The flash should be positioned opposite the main light source, off-camera at an angle of around 45 degrees. This will help to prevent red-eye, as well as giving a more natural feel to the artificial aspect of the source.

### Are there any disadvantages to using fill-in flash?

One of the advantages of a reflector is that reflected light can never be more powerful than the original source. Therefore reflected light never overpowers the primary light source. However, in a daylight studio it is entirely possible that the flash unit is more powerful than the main light source, which may become overwhelmed and 'drowned out' by the flash, with the likely result of spoiling your image.

**See also**

*Using fill-in flash with natural light (page 66)*

Off-camera flash

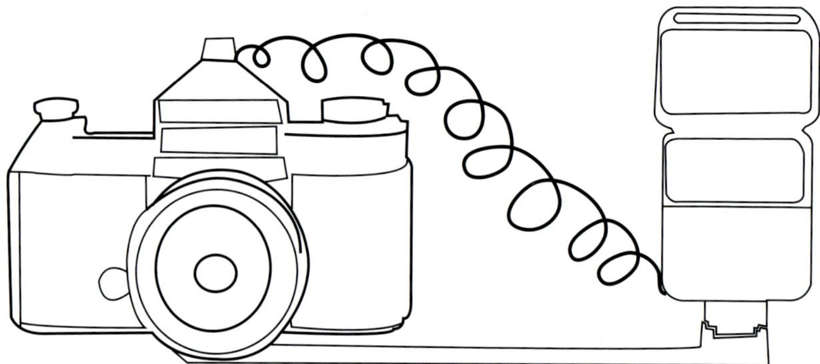

Flash units are typically best positioned off-camera, around 30–45 degrees to the subject.

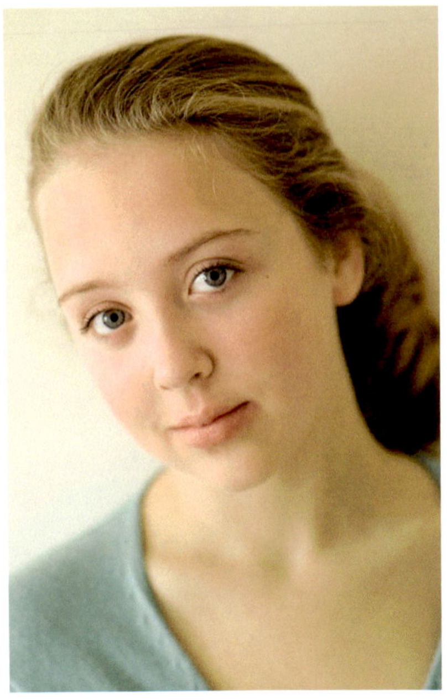

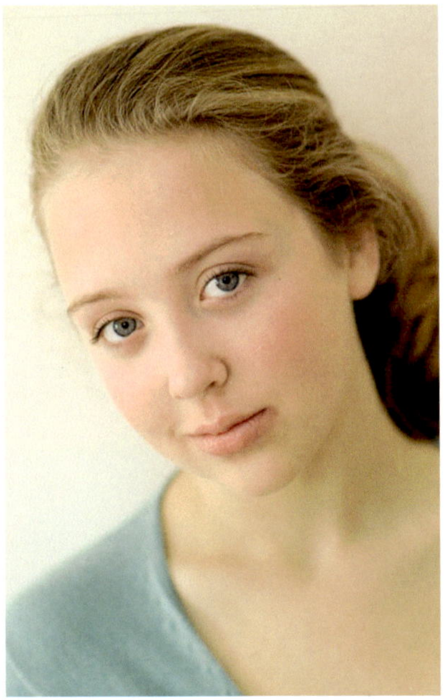

Fill-in flash has been used in the image on the right to help soften the shadows created by the primary light source (daylight).

## How do I meter when using fill-in flash?

The likelihood of the fill-in flash overpowering the main light source can be minimised if exposure is calculated correctly. The following steps illustrate how to calculate exposure using fill-in flash in a daylight studio environment:

**Step 1** Take a meter reading of the area lit by the main (primary) light source and make a note of the EV or suggested aperture/shutter speed settings.

**Step 2** Take a meter reading with a flash meter of the area lit by the flash unit, again noting the EV or exposure settings.

**Step 3** Calculate the difference between the two readings. If the flash meter reading has a higher EV than the daylight reading then the flash will overpower the principal source. Ideally the flash output should give a light level around 1 stop below that of the natural light source. To adjust the output of the flash you can either move the flash further away or reduce its power output.

**See also**

*Using fill-in flash with natural light (page 66)*

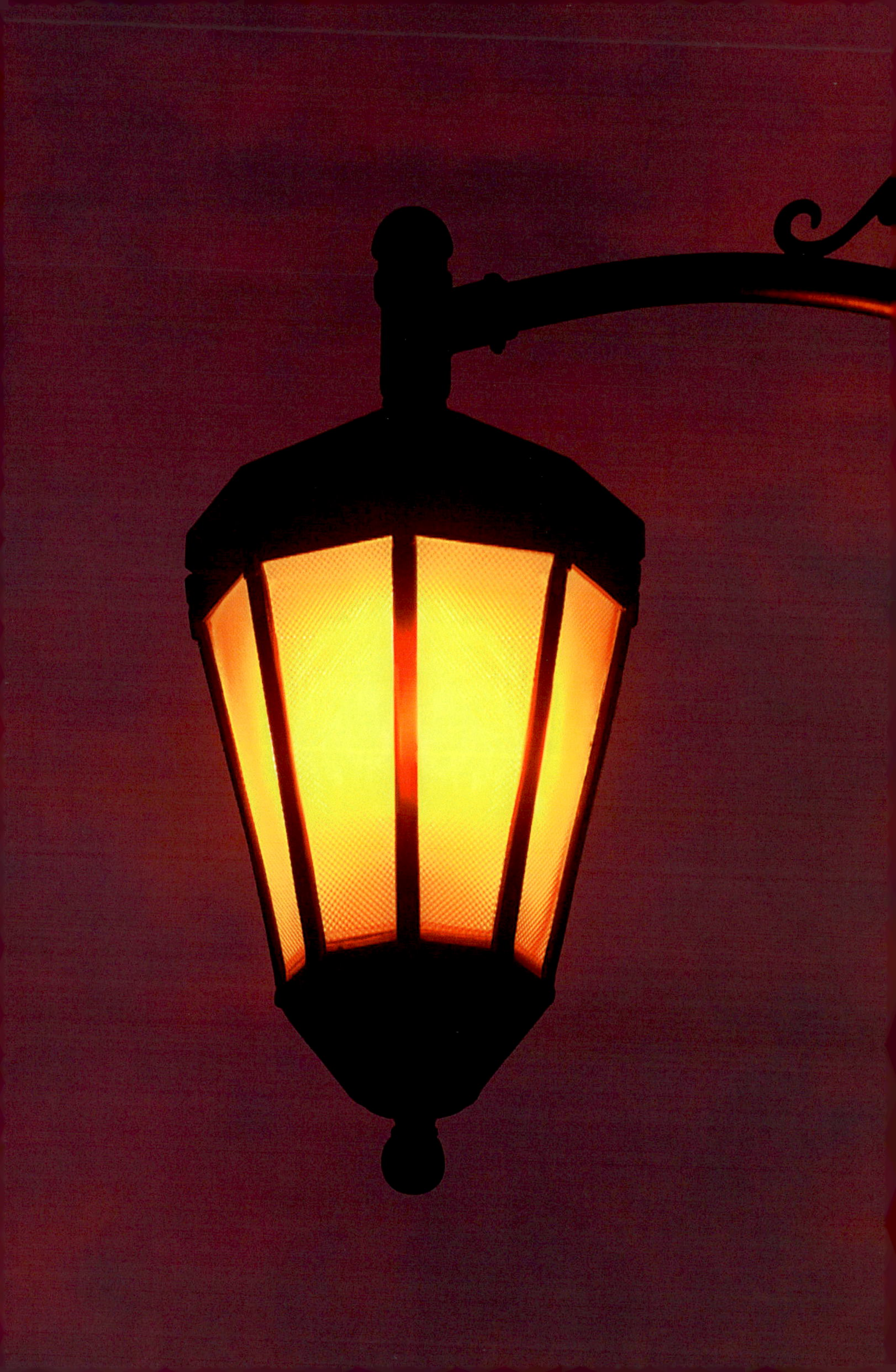

SECTION SEVEN

# ARTIFICIAL LIGHT

Artificial light provides photographers with the opportunity to extend their time in the field or to maximise creativity by controlling lighting conditions in a way that simply isn't possible with natural light.

However, using artificial light effectively takes knowledge and practice, especially given the high levels of sophistication of modern camera/flash systems. From understanding the different types of portable artificial light to knowing how best to deploy and use modern flash systems, the following chapter will help you get to grips with the skill base needed to create compelling images using artificial light.



Working with artificial light gives you greater control over the quality, direction and intensity of light.

# TYPES OF ARTIFICIAL LIGHTING

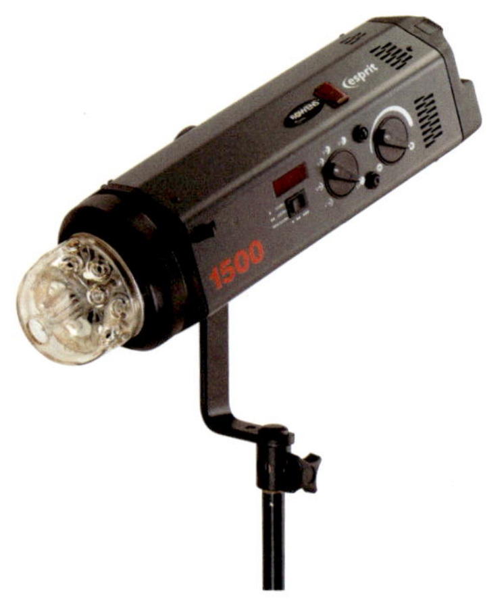

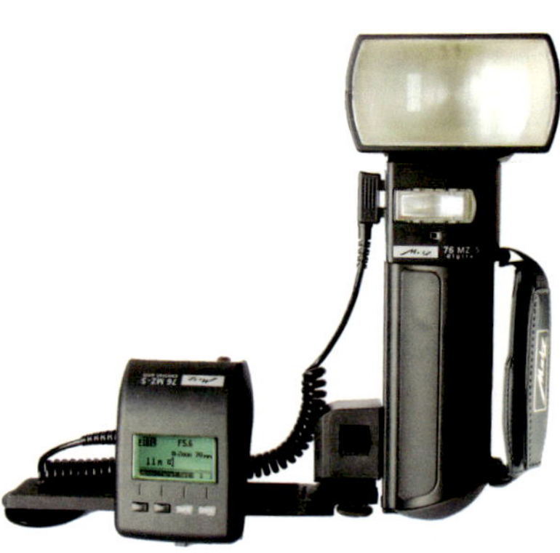

Flash units come in many guises, from large powerful studio lights to camera-attached units of varying sizes.

## What types of artificial lighting are available?

In photographic terms, when we talk about artificial light we almost always mean electronic flash, which does form the most popular type of artificial light. However, there are other forms of artificial lighting. In studios, in particular, continuous-source lighting from tungsten or fluorescent lamps may be employed. Professional photographers have even been known to occasionally use angle-poise desk lamps in their macro studios.

## What are the advantages of the different types of artificial light?

The obvious advantage of flash is its relative power compared to other types of artificial light. It is also balanced to match daylight, which makes life easier for film photographers used to shooting with daylight-balanced film. Electronic flash is also practically the only source of artificial light that can be used on-camera in the field.

Power can be a disadvantage of flash, particularly when shooting close to the subject, such as in macro photography, although this problem has largely been overcome by more sophisticated and relatively inexpensive portable flash units and specially designed macroflash units. The other disadvantage is the lack of any visual reference of the effects of flash lighting on the subject prior to exposure. When a continuous source lamp is used it is possible to see the effects of the light as it is moved or to change its power output before a picture is taken.

### See also

*Using flash in macro photography (page 86)*

### What is meant by the term 'portable flash lighting'?

In this book portable flash refers specifically to the self-contained flash units designed to work on-camera (either built-in or external) via the hot shoe or accessory shoe (this includes positioning such units off-camera on a flash bracket). Some studio flash systems are portable and used in the field, particularly by commercial, fashion and advertising photographers. However, these have been included under the following section on studio lighting.

### What types of portable artificial light are available?

There are four main types of portable flash unit available, although there are many variations on these. The simplest is the small pop-up flash that is built into many SLR cameras. Although very limited in their benefits, these units can be used to good effect if their limitations are taken into account. They can also be used effectively in some cases as a master flash to trigger more sophisticated off-camera units.

External flash units come in many and varied sizes but most have generic features, such as rotating and tilting heads and zoom capabilities. They are also more powerful than the built-in version. These units can be used on-camera, attached via the hot shoe mount, or off-camera on a bracket (or even hand-held) with a connecting cord. Today, these units tend to be dedicated to the camera. Small and portable, yet relatively powerful, these types of unit can provide excellent artificial light opportunities when used effectively.

The third type of portable flash is the hammerhead flash. These units can only be used off-camera with a bracket but are typically considerably more powerful than standard external units. Relatively large and heavy, they have the advantage of greater reach and quicker recycling times.

The fourth option is the macroflash, which is covered in more detail on pages 86–87.

There are many types of portable flash unit, the small but powerful external flashes being the most popular for general photography.

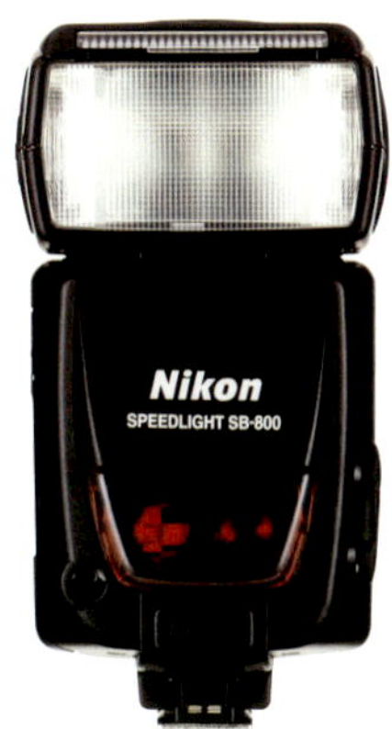


**See also**

*Choosing a portable flash unit (page 108)*
*Using flash in macro photography (page 86)*

# 37 ARTIFICIAL LIGHT
## CHOOSING A PORTABLE FLASH UNIT

### What are the main deciding factors in choosing a portable flash?

When looking to buy a portable flash unit one needs to consider five main aspects of flash systems: power, coverage, recycling time, flexibility and automation. Each of these is covered here in turn.

**Power**

Flash power, or output, is a measure of the quantity of light emitted by the unit, referred to by its guide number. The guide number indicates the maximum output of the flash, although it is possible with modern flash units to control output to levels below the maximum. In general terms the more powerful the unit the greater flexibility you have when setting exposures. For example, say you are photographing a subject and the closest you can get is 6 metres (20 feet) distant. If the maximum output of the flash gives a maximum shooting distance of 6 metres (20 feet) you will need to open the lens aperture to its maximum in order to maintain an accurate exposure because, in this example, you are unable to move the flash closer. However, with a more powerful flash you would be able to use apertures smaller than the maximum, giving you greater control over depth-of-field.

Flash coverage

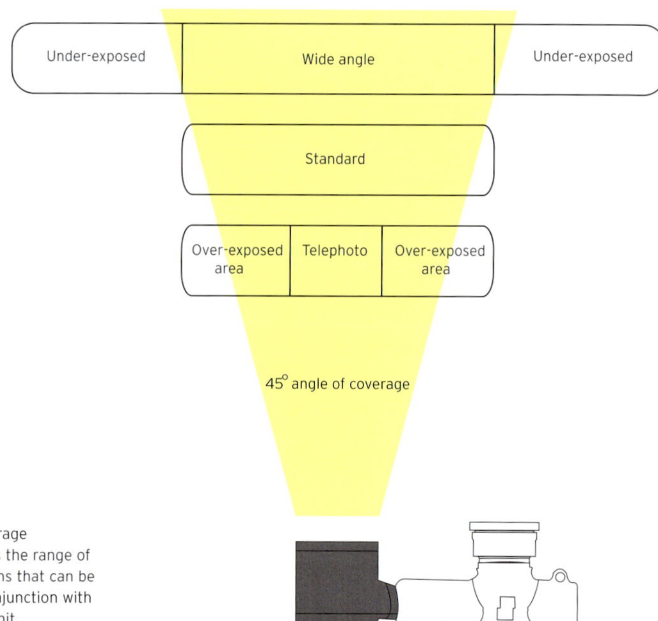


Flash coverage determines the range of focal lengths that can be used in conjunction with the flash unit.

**Coverage**
Flash coverage refers to the spread of the flash's light from the point source. Ideally this should match the angle of view of the lens used. For example, if the lens used has an angle of view of 22° then flash coverage needs to be equal. Most modern flash units have a built-in zoom head that enables changing of flash coverage to suit different lenses. However, there are some limitations, and older flash units may have a fixed coverage, typically matching a standard (50mm) lens.

The zoom coverage of most flash units ranges between 28mm and 135mm. The problem occurs when using lenses shorter or longer in focal length than covered by the zoom. If the lens used has a shorter focal length (e.g. 20mm) then the flash won't light some areas of the scene covered by the wide-angle lens and vignetting will occur. If the lens used has a longer focal length (e.g. 200mm), some of the light from the flash will be lost but may be taken into account by the metering system, resulting in over-exposure of the subject.

Again the same rule applies as for power. The wider the coverage the more flexibility you have, in this case when deciding on composition and perspective.

**See also**

*Flash accessories (page 112)*

**Recycling time**
Recycling time refers to the speed at which the flash unit recharges after discharge. Modern flash units no longer fully discharge every time they are fired. Instead, an exact amount of light necessary to attain an accurate exposure is emitted. This has significantly reduced flash recycling times, which can be less than a second. However, recycling times are important when multiple images are taken in quick succession, for example in sports and wildlife photography.

**Flexibility**
The pop-up flash on the camera lacks flexibility in that not only is its position fixed, but so too is the angle of the head. Modern flash units tend to enable a certain amount of swivel and tilt movement, which allows for the use of bounced flash. This flexibility increases the ability to alter the quality of light from a unit.

**Tip**

*It's possible to increase coverage range, although sometimes at the expense of output. For example, a diffuser will broaden the coverage of the flash but reduce illumination by around 1 stop. And a flash extender will enable use of longer focal length lenses than that catered for by the unit's zoom function.*

**See also**

*Quality of light (page 24)*

**Automation**
Modern flash units take a lot of information from the camera, including flash-to-subject distance (calculated from lens focus distance) and exposure information (using the TTL-AE system). This has greatly reduced the need to manually calculate flash exposures. As with automated cameras these things have a time and a place and it is still recommended that you learn how to do things manually even if eventually you resort to relying on the camera. However, what automation brings is the flexibility to decide what is best for any given situation.

**See also**

*Flash exposure (page 120)*

**What is a Guide Number (GN)?**

A flash unit's Guide Number (GN) indicates its power output in relation to a standard film speed or digital ISO setting. The higher the guide number, the more powerful the flash. This number is usually indicated in the owner's manual, represented, for example, in a statement such as GN = X at ISO 100.

The Guide Number is important when calculating flash exposures manually, as it is used in the formula for calculating flash-to-subject distance or lens aperture.

**Tip**

*A common technique used to sell flash units is to quote guide numbers for higher ISO ratings, giving the impression of a more powerful unit. For example, a flash unit with a guide number of 120 quoted for ISO 400 seems, on the face of it, a powerful flash. However, it is less powerful than a unit with a guide number of 40 for ISO 25. So, when comparing the power of different flash units always ensure that the ISO rating used is consistent.*

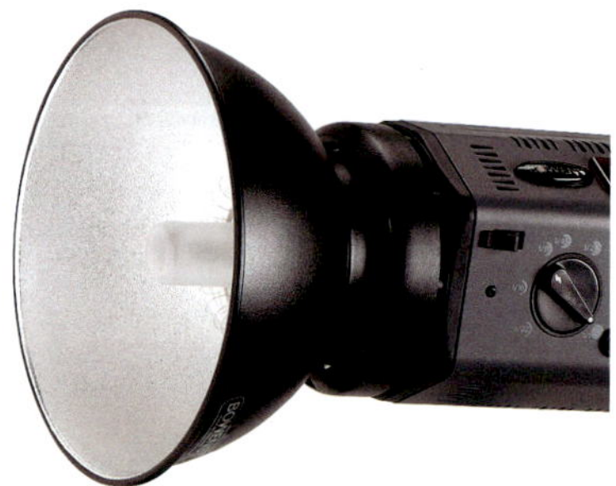

The power of a flash unit is given as a Guide Number. Understanding how to relate this to flash output is important when investing in expensive flash equipment.

## What is a dedicated flash?

The most evolved form of flash unit is the dedicated flash. These units are designed to work with specific brands of camera and take all the necessary information they need to calculate exposure from the camera and lens. The aim of the manufacturers was to make flash photography easier and more accurate and, in many ways, they have achieved this. However, as with any automated system in photography a correct exposure is not necessarily the desired exposure. Dedicated flash units can only be used on the cameras they were designed for. For example, a Nikon dedicated flash couldn't be used on a Pentax camera, and vice versa.

## Can I use non-proprietary flash systems?

Several of the non-proprietary flash manufacturers, such as Metz, produce systems designed to work with certain brands of camera. For example, it is possible to get Metz flash units dedicated to Nikon digital SLR cameras. On the whole non-proprietary systems will work equally effectively, although very rarely some anomalies may occur.

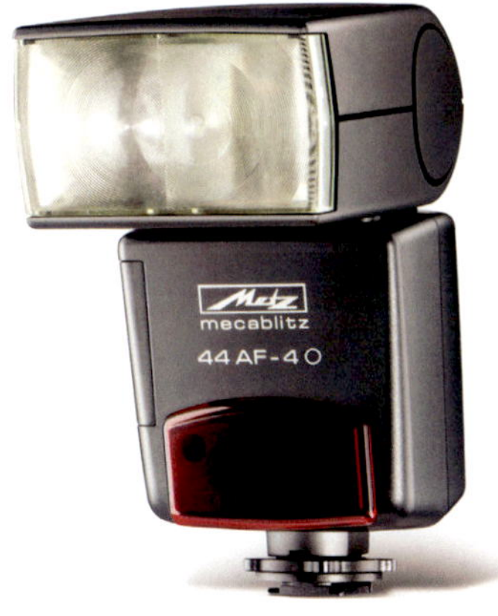


Non-proprietary flash units are available that operate efficiently with the camera's dedicated flash computers.

## Can I use my manual flash with a digital camera?

By calculating flash exposure manually it's possible to use a manual flash with a digital camera. However, automated flash and dedicated flash units need to be designed specifically to work with digital cameras due to the different ways that film and digital sensors record light. Most camera manufacturers now produce dedicated flash units especially for digital cameras.

# FLASH ACCESSORIES

## What is a portable flash diffuser?

A portable flash diffuser fits over the flash head and scatters emitted light, turning the hard direct light of the flash into a softer-quality light. Some flash units are sold with a dedicated diffuser; otherwise it's possible to buy non-proprietary diffusers made by companies such as Sto-fen.

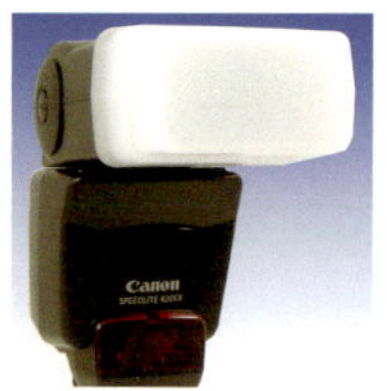

A diffuser can be used with a portable flash unit to soften the quality of light.

## What is a flash extender?

Flash extenders are designed to be used with long focal length lenses of 300mm or longer. A precision Fresnel lens concentrates the flash's light, providing for up to 3 stops of additional illumination. Extenders are invaluable when it's impossible to get close enough to the subject for flash to operate effectively, such as in wildlife and sports photography.

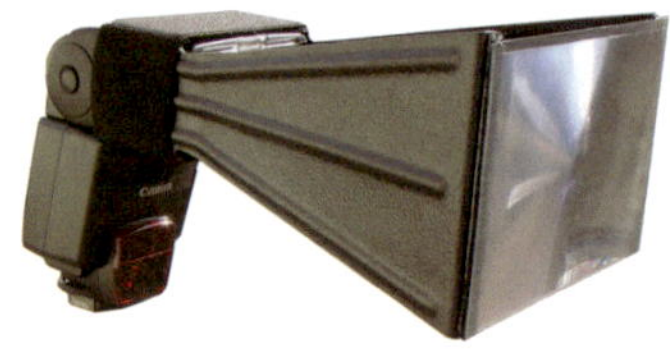

A flash extender can be used to increase the range of the flash.

## When would I use an off-camera shoe cord?

When the flash is attached to the hot shoe on the camera, information is passed between the camera and the flash unit. When the flash is removed for off-camera work, a shoe cord connects to the hot shoe and the flash and acts as a conduit for the continued passing of information. Without this accessory flash automation would be lost when the flash was used off-camera.

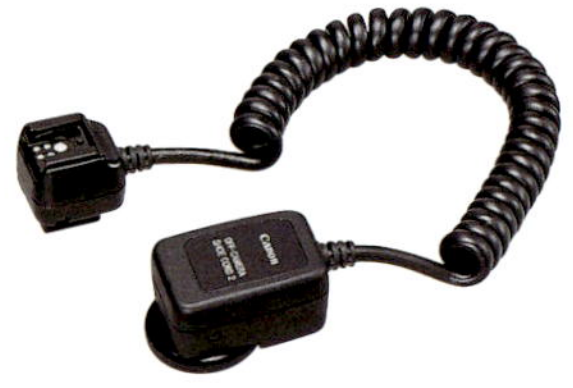

Full automation can be maintained when the camera is positioned off-camera by using a flash connecting cord.

## What's the purpose of a flash bracket?

A flash bracket is used to support the flash unit off-camera. Several types of bracket are available, including very inexpensive straight brackets that simply hold the flash in a single, fixed position. More expensive and sophisticated designs are available that enable the flash to be positioned in one of several different ways.

**See also**

*Quality of light (page 24)*

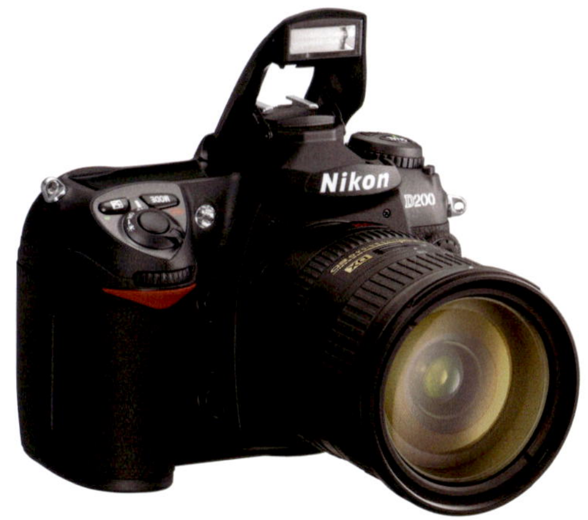


The small built-in pop-up flash units on cameras are limited in their power and coverage but can be utilised to good effect in certain instances.

## How effective is my camera's built-in pop-up flash?

The small flash units built into cameras are designed mainly for point-and-shoot snapshot photography. They are low-powered, compared to external units, with a relatively low Guide Number, and their position is fixed. Being directly above the lens is also the worst place to position a flash in the majority of cases.

That said, they do have their advantages. For example, they can be used as a master flash to trigger more powerful off-camera units. Their low power, in this case, is advantageous in that the light they emit won't impinge greatly on exposures. It is also sometimes effective to use the pop-up flash in your back-up camera to add a catchlight to an animal's eyes when photographing wildlife on dull days.

### Tip

*To soften the quality of light from a pop-up camera flash, cover the flash head with a thin white cloth, such as a handkerchief, which will act as a diffuser.*

## Can I change the quality of light from my built-in flash?

Actually yes, you can, although the method of doing so is a little ad-hoc. Covering the flash head with a piece of thin cloth, such as a cotton handkerchief, and securing it with an elastic band will diffuse the light emitted by the unit. Another useful trick is to carry a packet of Rizla papers, using a single paper attached to the top of the flash housing rolled in front of the flash head to act as a diffuser. (The blue Rizla papers work the best!)

### See also

*Choosing a portable flash unit (page 108)*

**What are the advantages of using an external flash unit?**

External flash units have two distinct advantages over pop-up units. Firstly they tend to be more powerful, enabling greater flexibility in camera position relative to the subject and exposure settings. Secondly, being off-camera they can be positioned at an angle suitable to the subject.

Additionally, multiple units can be used in unison for more creative lighting effects. Other advantages include greater coverage and faster recycling times.

A built-in pop-up flash has been used in the image below (top) to brighten the overall exposure of this image of blossom.

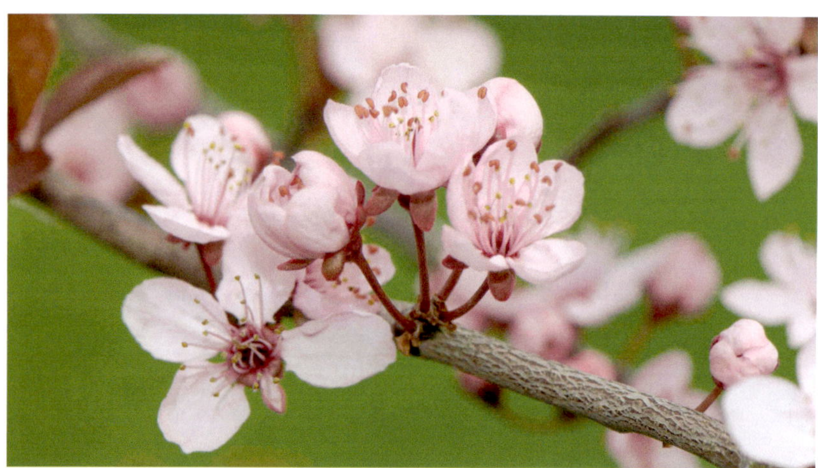

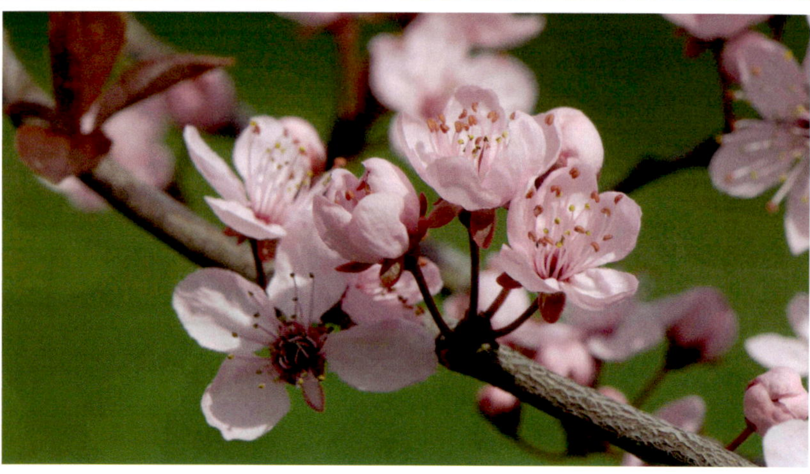

## How do modern wireless multiple flash systems work?

Recent years have seen the introduction of sophisticated wireless multiple flash systems, such as Nikon's i-TTL flash system. With these systems it is possible to employ several remote flash units all controlled from a master unit, with data transmitted (usually) via infrared light.

In many ways, these systems are revolutionary. Previously, to create such a flash set-up would have required lots of wires and lengthy exposure calculations. Now it is more simply a case of positioning the flash units as required and letting the system automatically determine appropriate exposure and flash output for all units. If necessary, individual or groups of flash units can be adjusted to alter flash output wirelessly from a master unit.

Wireless multiple flash systems

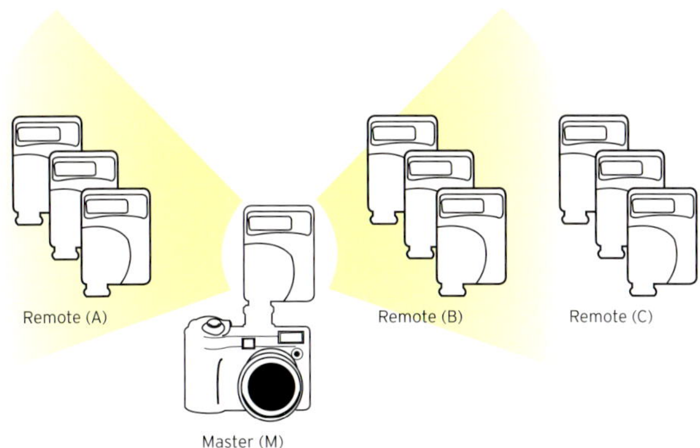


## Should I invest in a wireless multiple flash system?

That depends on the type of photography you intend doing. As with anything this sophisticated the systems aren't cheap. For example, a basic two-unit set-up using the Nikon system will cost a minimum of £300/$600 and double that when using the more powerful SB-800 units. A four-unit set-up will relieve your wallet of over £1,000/$2,000.

On the other hand, if your photography requires significant use of artificial lighting in creative ways then these systems provide the flexibility of studio lighting with added portability.

Flash is getting ever more sophisticated. Most camera manufacturers now produce simple to use, creative multiple flash systems that can operate wirelessly.

**See also**

*Suggested studio light set-ups (page 139)*

# POSITIONING THE FLASH UNIT

### Should I use the hot shoe on the camera for attaching external flash units?

Generally, using the hot shoe for attaching an external flash unit should be avoided, as the direct frontal lighting that will result is often unflattering to a subject. This is less of an issue if you are bouncing the flash's light off a ceiling or wall, or using a diffuser to soften the quality of the light.

When using the flash in an unaltered state it is better to position the flash unit off-camera at an angle between 30 and 60 degrees and slightly above eye level. The angled lighting will help to create shadows that accentuate form and the raised position will better mimic sunlight.

### What is the most common position for flash?

Typically an external flash unit is positioned at around 45 degrees to the subject, although there are no hard and fast rules governing flash position. What is important is to understand the relationship between flash position and contrast, and how this affects the visual rendition of the subject on paper or on screen.

**See also**

*Direction of light (page 28)*

**Positioning the flash unit**

The 'favourite' flash position is an angle around 30–45 degrees to the subject, positioned slightly above eye level.

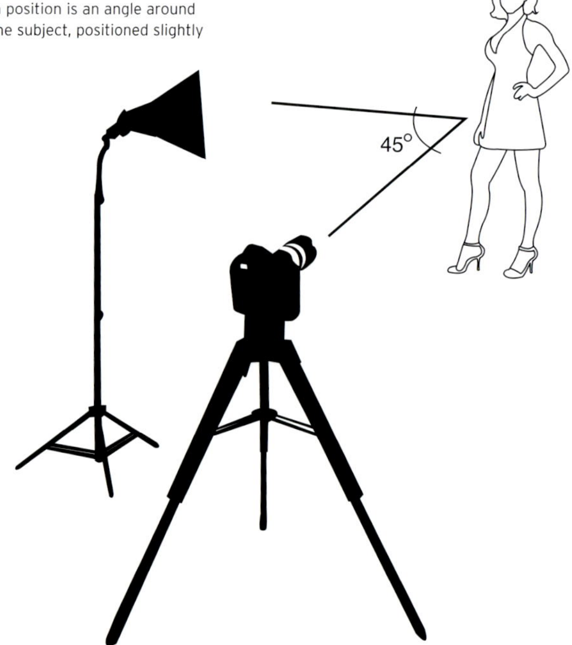

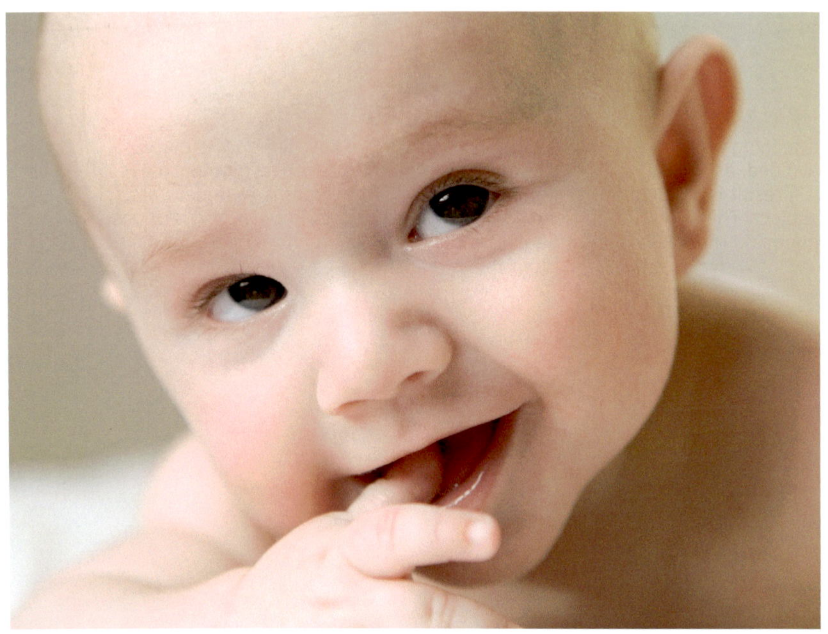

Great images are possible with just a single flash unit.

### Can I get great images with a single flash unit?

While multiple flash units increase creative possibilities, using a single flash head shouldn't be discounted. For example, mixing primary flash with ambient natural light can produce very good results, with the ambient light acting here as the fill-light to lift shadow areas created by the primary flash.

With a single, portable flash it's important to keep the unit relatively close to the subject so that it's not operating at maximum capacity for each shot. This will increase the range of exposure settings that can be set.

Other options with a single flash are to bounce or otherwise soften the light and use reflectors to fill in shadow areas.

### How would a reflector improve the image?

Reflectors are used to redirect light back on to a subject to lighten shadow areas. The result is less dramatic contrast and softer lighting. The advantage of a reflector is that reflected light can never be brighter than the main source light. The differential in light quality and/or intensity helps to give form to a subject.

**See also**

*Panel reflectors and diffusers (page 49)*
*Suggested studio light set-ups (page 139)*

Reflectors help to add light in shadow areas without overpowering the primary light source. They are an essential accessory in studio photography.

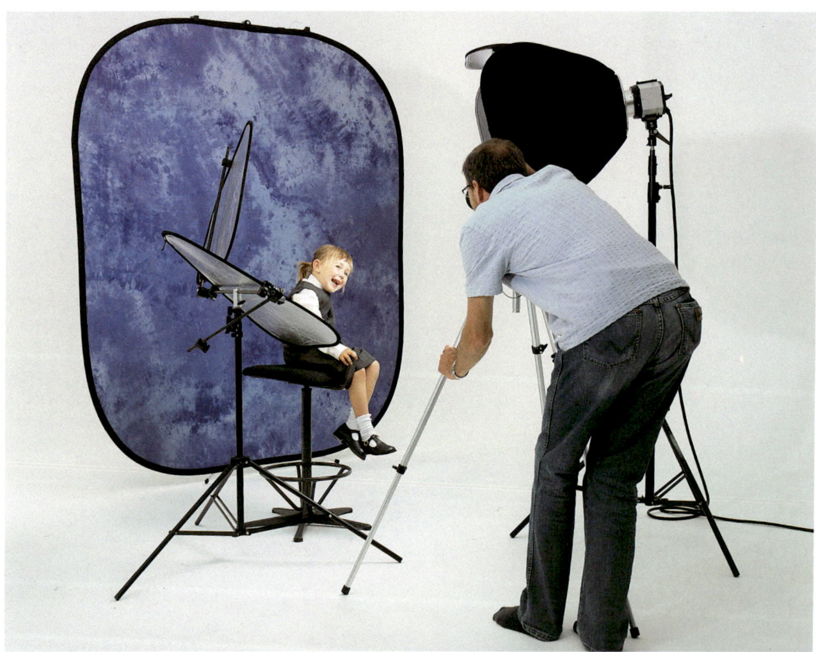

### How do I change the direction of light from a portable flash?

Many portable flash units have a swivel and tilt head that enables emitted light to be bounced off a nearby wall or ceiling, thus changing the direction of light. However, this will also soften the quality of light, which may not be the intention. If the flash unit is used off-camera, simply altering its position will change the direction of light. For example, move it 90 degrees from front and frontal lighting becomes side lighting. A further 90 degrees and you have back lighting.

If the camera is in a fixed position off-camera then consider changing the position of the subject, relative to the flash unit.

**See also**

*Direction of light (page 28)*

### How can I change the quality of light from a portable flash unit?

Unaltered flash lighting is considered hard in quality. Its quality can be changed to soft lighting by using a diffuser in front of the flash head, or by bouncing the light from a wall or ceiling.

**See also**

*Quality of light (page 24)*

### What type of surface can I use to bounce flash?

The reflective surface should be white and preferably uncoloured, as colours will also change the actual colour of the reflected light (unless this is your aim). Sometimes silver and gold are used instead of white. Silver produces more contrast than white, and gold will create a warm colour cast. Many photographers prefer to bounce light from a ceiling rather than a wall as the resulting angle is a closer match to the angle of sunlight, giving a more natural effect. As well as walls and ceilings, any flat reflective surface can be used.

**Tip**

*The laws of physics state that the angle of reflectance is equal to the angle of incidence. That is, light will reflect from a surface at the same angle it hits the surface. This is important to consider when deciding on the angle of the flash.*

### What is the bounced-flash technique?

Bouncing flash simply means directing the flash head at a reflective subject, such as a wall or ceiling. When the flash is fired the light first hits this surface and is then reflected and scattered with some of the reflected light falling on the subject. The aim is to turn a small point light source into a large omni-directional source, reducing contrast by softening light quality.

When using bounced flash you need to consider the overall distance the light travels in order to calculate a correct exposure. For example, if the distance between the flash and the reflective surface is, say, 4 metres (13 feet) and the distance between the reflective surface and the subject is 3 metres (10 feet) then the total flash-to-subject distance is 7 metres (23 feet).

One consequence of bounced flash is absorption – the amount of light absorbed by the surface and the scattering of the light waves. This will necessitate compensation in exposure to account for the loss of light caused by absorption.

To calculate the relevant exposure compensation first set and maintain camera position (e.g. using a tripod). Take a flash meter reading with the flash directed at the subject. Now set the flash position to bounce the flash's light and take another flash meter reading. The difference in EV between the two readings is your absorption (compensation) factor. For example, if the first flash meter reading gives an EV of 8 and the bounced-flash flash meter reading gives an EV of 7 then the loss of light caused by absorption equates to 1 stop.

**See also**

*Flash exposure (page 120)*

# 42 ARTIFICIAL LIGHT
## FLASH EXPOSURE

### How do I calculate exposure when using portable flash?

Practically all modern flash units, particularly the dedicated variety, are designed to produce technically accurate exposures automatically, even when using multiple flash set-ups. However, if you are using non-automated flash understanding the process to calculate flash exposure manually is necessary and important.

Flash exposure is based on flash-to-subject distance, which is determined by the Guide Number and ISO rating of the film or ISO setting of the sensor. To calculate the GN for varying ISO ratings follow these steps:

**Step 1** Note the base GN and ISO rating given by the manufacturer. For example, this may be given as GN=80 at ISO 100. (These details should be in the owner's manual; alternatively you may find them on the Web.)

**Step 2** For the purpose of the calculation we're going to revert to working with the f/stop scale. Drop the zero (divide by 10) from 80 (the GN) to give you 8, read as f/8.

**Step 3** Calculate the difference in stops of the working ISO rating. For example, if you are calculating the GN for ISO 400 then the difference in stops will be 2 stops.

**Step 4** Going back to the f/stop scale calculate minus 2 stops from f/8 (because of the faster ISO rating), giving you f/16. Now add back the nought dropped in Step 2 (multiply by 10) and you have a Guide Number of 160 at ISO 400.

Once you have the GN at the working ISO rating it's possible to calculate flash exposure manually using the following formulas:

**To calculate flash-to-subject distance:**

$$\text{Flash-to-subject distance (FSD)} = \frac{\text{guide number (GN)}}{\text{lens aperture (LA)}}$$

E.g. 160 (GN) / 8 (LA) = 20 metres (FSD)

**To calculate lens aperture if FSD is fixed:**

$$\text{Lens aperture (LA)} = \frac{\text{guide number (GN)}}{\text{flash-to-subject distance (FSD)}}$$

E.g. 160 (GN) / 20 metres (FSD) = 8 (lens aperture)

Flash-to-subject distance

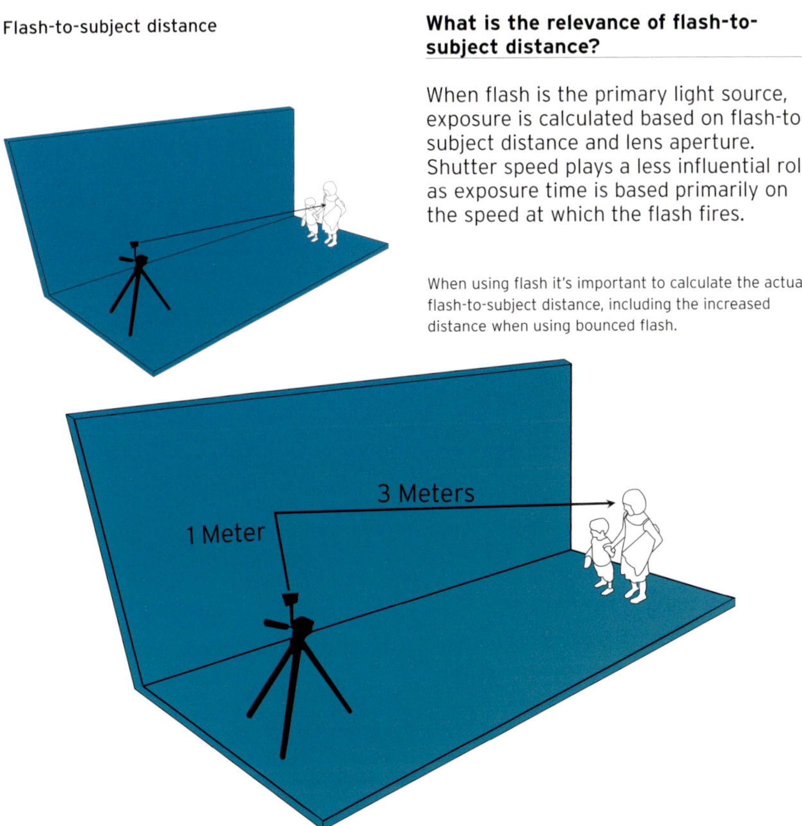


## What is the relevance of flash-to-subject distance?

When flash is the primary light source, exposure is calculated based on flash-to-subject distance and lens aperture. Shutter speed plays a less influential role as exposure time is based primarily on the speed at which the flash fires.

When using flash it's important to calculate the actual flash-to-subject distance, including the increased distance when using bounced flash.

## How do I calculate exposure when using bounced or diffused flash?

To calculate exposure manually for bounced flash, simply use the calculations given opposite (How do I calculate exposure when using portable flash?) and then apply the absorption factor described on page 119 (What is the bounced flash technique?).

For example, taking the example used above:

$$\text{Lens aperture (LA)} = \frac{\text{guide number (GN)}}{\text{flash-to-subject distance (FSD)}}$$

E.g. 160 (GN) / 20 metres (FSD) = 8 (lens aperture)

Then apply the absorption factor of say -1 stop giving a flash exposure of:

E.g. 160 (GN) / 20 metres (FSD) = 8 (lens aperture) minus 1 stop = f/5.6

# 43 ARTIFICIAL LIGHT
## CAMERA SETTINGS FOR FLASH PHOTOGRAPHY

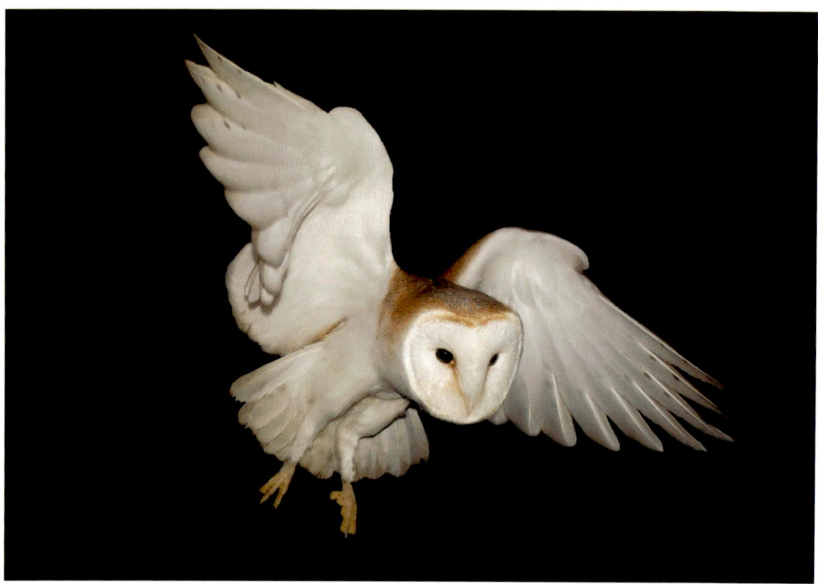

When flash is the sole light source, the speed of the flash output becomes the effective shutter speed, irrespective of the shutter speed set on the camera itself.

### Why is shutter speed less influential in flash photography?

When flash is used as the primary light source the subject is exposed only so long as it is lit. In this instance it is the duration of the flash emitted that becomes the effective shutter speed. However, when used in conjunction with ambient light, shutter speed will affect how peripheral objects are exposed.


**See also**

*Advanced flash photography techniques (page 124)*


### What is flash sync shutter speed?

Flash sync speed refers to the fastest shutter speed you can use with flash. Using shutter speeds in excess of the sync speed will result either in a partial blackout of the image (with older cameras) or, with modern cameras, overriding of the set shutter speed to the flash sync speed.

### What White Balance setting should I use with flash?

Light from a flash unit has a Kelvin temperature close to daylight around noon on a sunny day. Most digital cameras have a pre-set WB setting specifically for electronic flash. It is equally OK to set WB to the pre-set Daylight setting.

### Is there a special film I should use for flash photography?

Because of the closeness in Kelvin temperature between flash light and daylight it is acceptable to use daylight-balanced film for flash photography under normal circumstances.

### What are the different flash sync modes?

Modern cameras have various settings for flash synchronisation modes. The standard setting is front-curtain sync. In this setting the flash fires as the shutter curtain opens at the beginning of the exposure. When rear-curtain sync mode is selected, the flash fires at the end of the exposure, rather than at the beginning. For more about how to use these settings, see Advanced flash photography techniques (page 124). Another option, also described on page 124, is slow-sync flash mode, which enables very slow shutter speeds (less than 1/60 second) to be used with flash.

### Should I use flash bracketing?

Flash bracketing performs the same role as standard exposure bracketing. Multiple images of the scene are captured at exposures over- and under-exposed from the metered exposure. The purpose is to ensure at least one accurate exposure. The advantage of flash bracketing is it reduces the likelihood of missing an important image due to incorrect exposure. The disadvantages are an increase in film costs, for film cameras only, and it is a technique that is less effective with moving subjects, as the composition between exposures may change significantly.

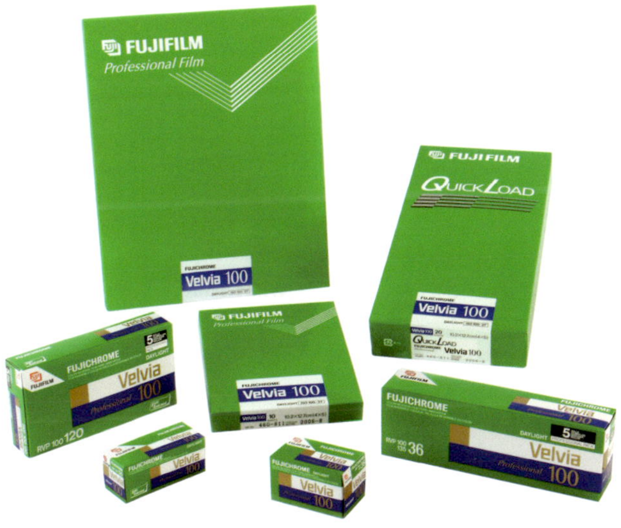


Daylight-balanced film is appropriate to use with flash, as the light output from most flash units has a Kelvin value very close to daylight.

## What is the purpose of slow-sync flash mode?

In many cameras the slowest factory set shutter speed that can be used with flash is around 1/60 second. In many situations this is an adequate shutter speed setting. However, at 1/60 second anything other than very bright ambient light will underexpose. This has the effect, for example, of leaving poorly lit background and peripheral objects overly dark and lacking detail.

When slow-sync flash mode is set, shutter speeds slower than 1/60 second and up to around 30 seconds can be used. The longer exposure times enable more ambient light to be exposed, brightening background and peripheral detail for a more balanced image.

Setting rear-curtain sync (opposite, right) creates a blur of motion behind the subject (where you would expect to see it). In normal sync mode the blur would appear in front of the subject and appear very unnatural.

Slow-sync flash can be used with slow shutter speeds to create interesting aesthetic effects.

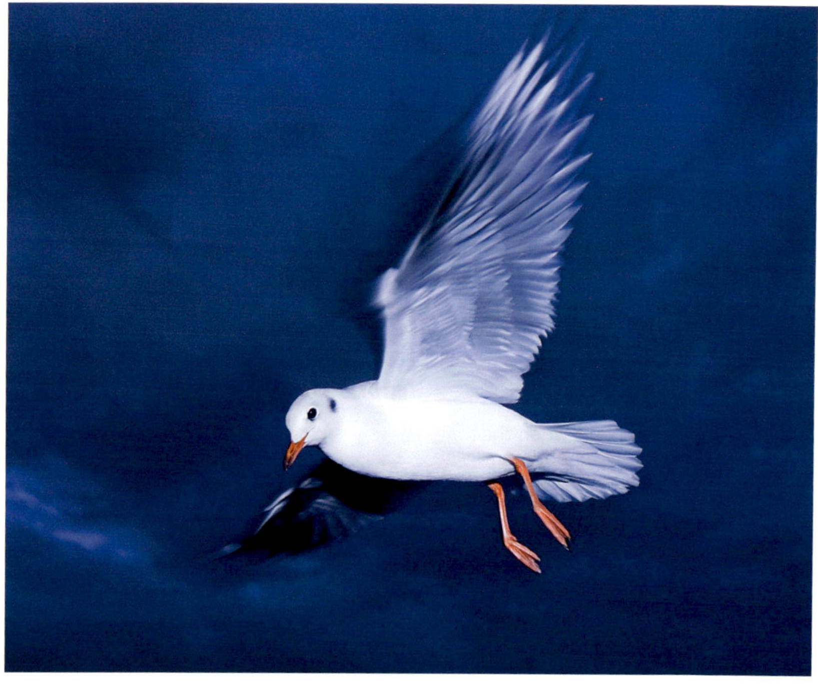

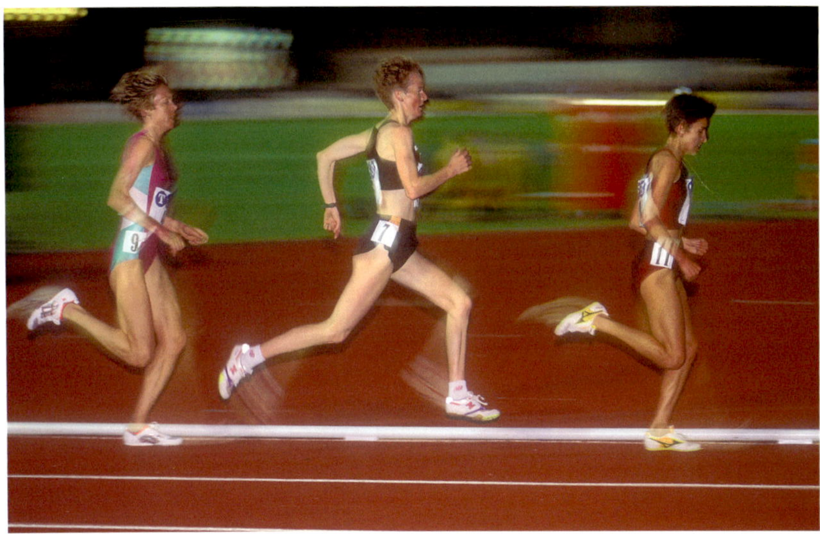

### When would I use rear-curtain flash sync mode?

Under normal circumstances a flash will fire at the moment the front curtain is at the beginning of its optimum opening, referred to as front-curtain sync. This has the effect of freezing motion at the beginning of the exposure. Front-curtain sync is adequate for most flash photography. However, when making long exposures and using flash, front-curtain sync creates an effect where the motion blur appears unnaturally in front of the subject.

To combat this, some cameras provide the ability to fire the flash when the shutter is at the end of its optimum opening. This is called rear-curtain sync, and it is used to freeze motion at the end of the exposure. Thus, when making long exposures and using flash, rear-curtain sync creates the effect of motion blur appearing behind the subject, where you'd expect it to be.

### What is high-speed flash?

As mentioned earlier, flash sync speed, in many cameras, is set to around a maximum of 1/250 second. Some high-specification cameras now provide a high-speed flash sync (or FP) facility, which enables the flash to be used at shutter speeds up to the maximum camera setting (sometimes in excess of 1/4,000 second). High speed flash sync mode can be used with extremely fast-moving subjects to help freeze motion, when ambient light would otherwise cause an amount of subject blur.

# AVOIDING THE PITFALLS OF PORTABLE FLASH

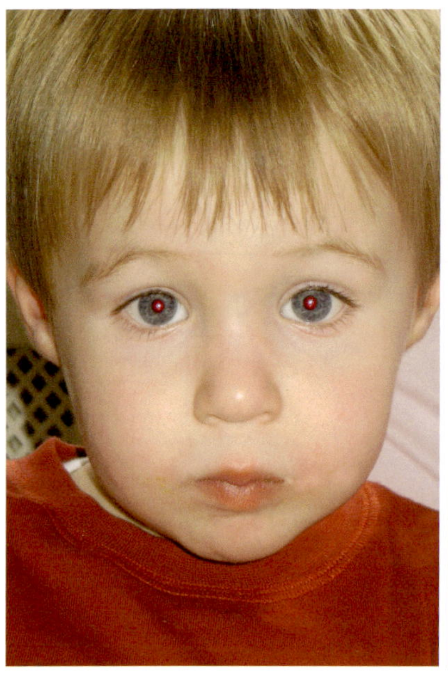

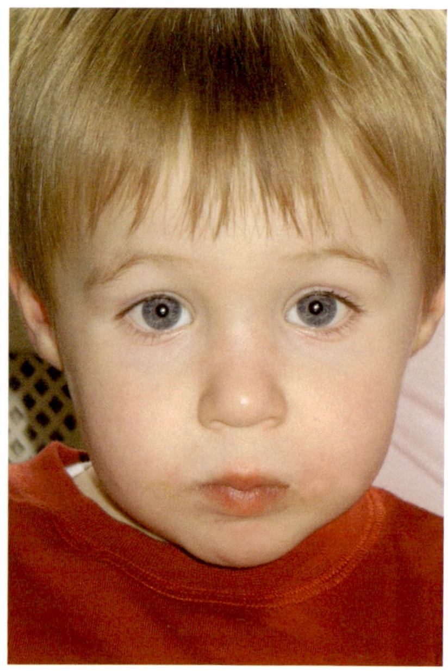

Red-eye, caused by light reflecting directly off the retina of the eye (left), can give subjects a very unnatural look. Using off-camera flash solves this problem (right).

## How can I avoid red-eye?

Human and some animal subjects when photographed with flash positioned directly in front of them are likely to suffer from a phenomenon known as red-eye, which is caused by light reflecting directly off the retina of the eye. The best way to avoid red-eye is to position the flash at an angle relative to the subject. Alternatively, diffusing the flash will reduce the likelihood of red-eye occurring. Some cameras have a flash sync mode known as red-eye reduction, which is supposed to minimise the effects of red-eye. While this works in limited circumstances, there is no better way of avoiding red-eye than keeping the flash off-camera.

### How can I avoid dark distinct shadows?

Harsh shadows are caused by hard, direct lighting. Diffusing the light emitted from the flash using a diffuser or by bouncing the light off a reflective surface will soften the quality of light and shadows. Alternatively, using a reflector or fill-in flash to lift the shadow areas will reduce contrast and soften shadows.

**See also**

*Flash exposure (page 120)*
*Panel reflectors and diffusers (page 49)*

Hard lighting from a direct source causes intense shadows. Softening the light with a diffuser isn't always an option, in which case fill-in flash or waiting for different weather conditions are possible solutions.

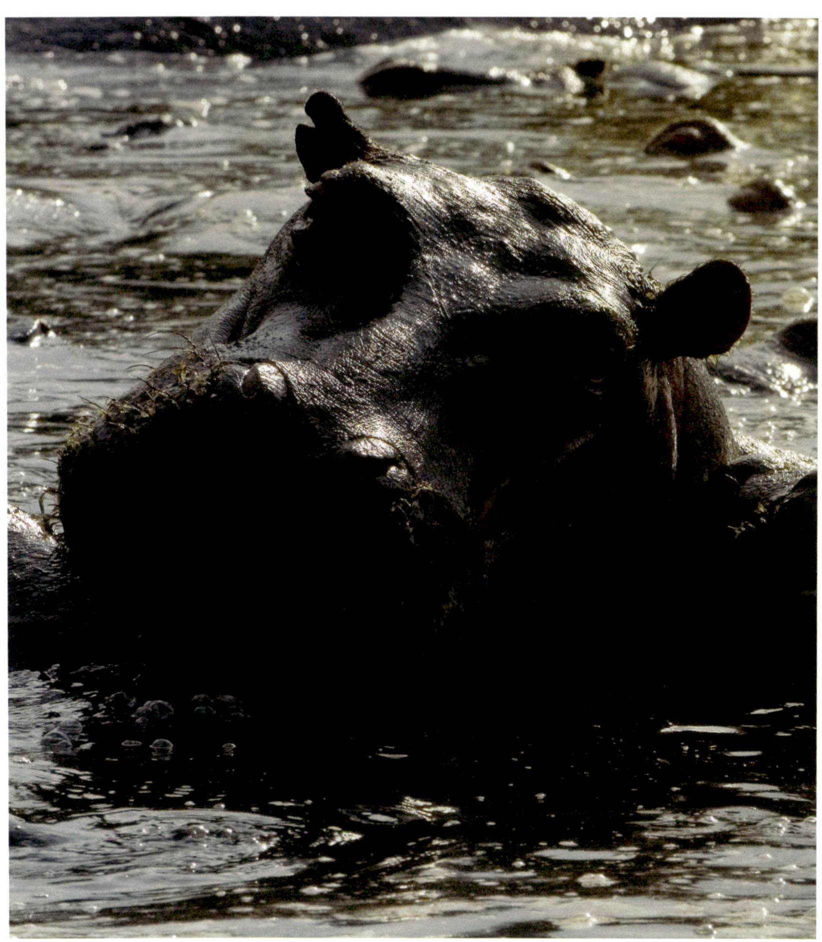

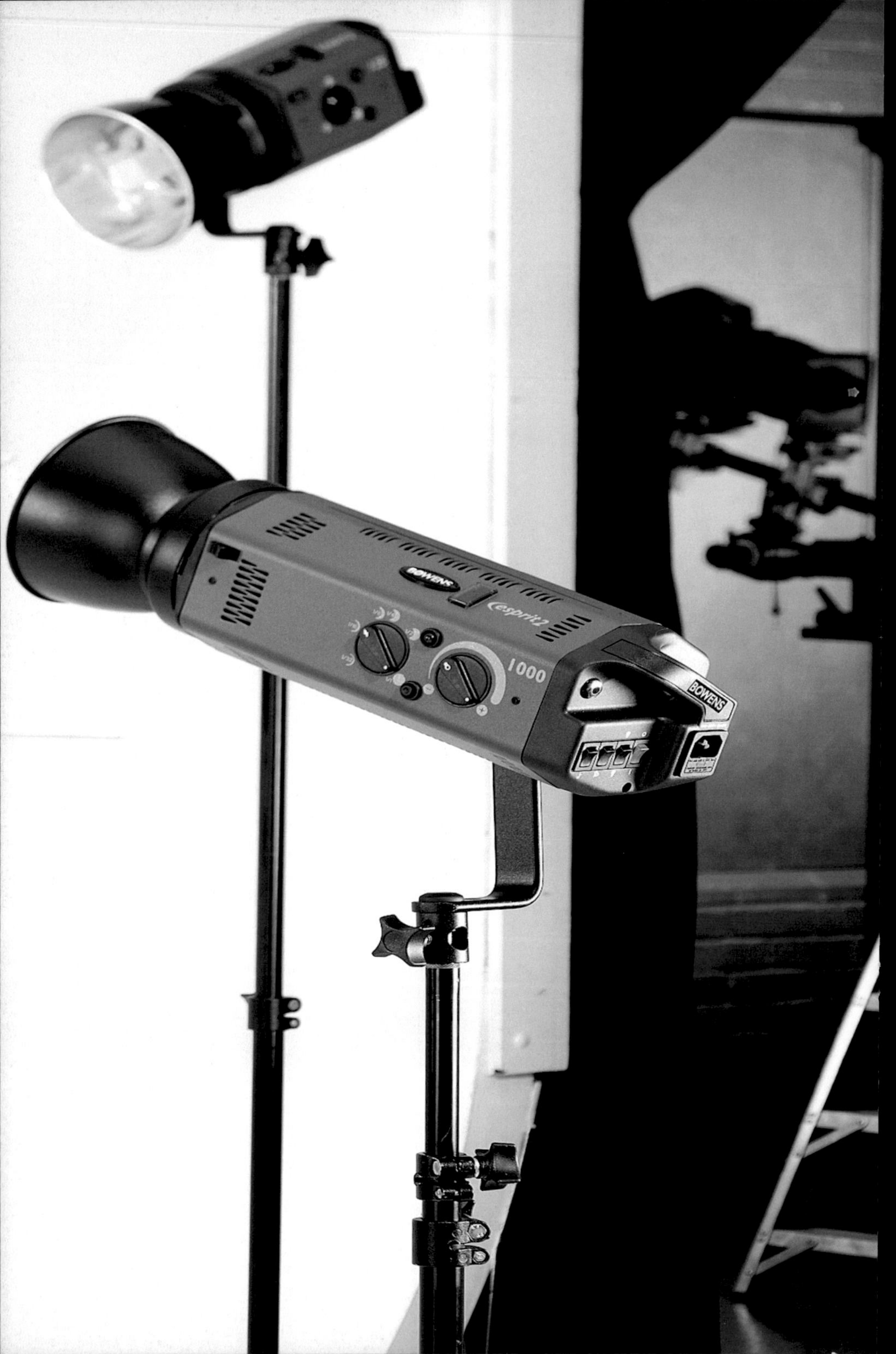
BOWENS
esprit2
1000
BOWENS

SECTION EIGHT

# ARTIFICIAL STUDIO LIGHTING

It is in the studio that photographers have the greatest degree of control over lighting. Here photographs can be constructed from scratch in much the same way an artist creates a painting.

When contemplating studio lighting it is important to understand the relationship between the lighting unit and the attachments, which resembles that of the relationship between a camera and a lens. A camera is, to all intents and purposes, a light-tight box that holds a piece of film or a sensor, and it is the lens that controls the image and perspective. So it is that a studio flash simply emits light; it's the attachments that control perspective and artistry.

The following chapter deals mainly with this aspect of studio lighting and, while not ignoring the technical aspects of the light, deals mainly with how to achieve the results you desire.



In the studio, complete control over lighting gives the photographer the ability to conjure an image from scratch.

# SIMPLE STUDIO LIGHTING

## Is there an inexpensive way to start in studio photography?

Go into a professional photographic studio and you'll quickly see that it is possible to spend more money on lighting than on cameras and lenses. However, this needn't be the case when starting out.

A single studio flash with a complementary range of attachments will get you started, if you know how to use them. A two-unit set-up will give you more options and three or four units even more. But there is much to be said for learning your trade with a simple, less complex set-up that challenges you to get the most out of limited equipment.

Look through the catalogues of some of the better-known lighting companies and you'll find some good, inexpensive starter kits. For example, Elinchrom produces a studio starter kit with two lights and various reflectors, umbrellas and stands for around £200/$400. Interfit offers a similar product for a similar price, and there will be others.

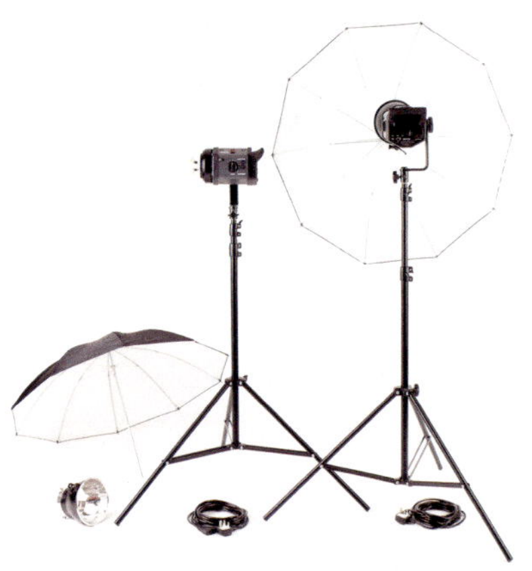

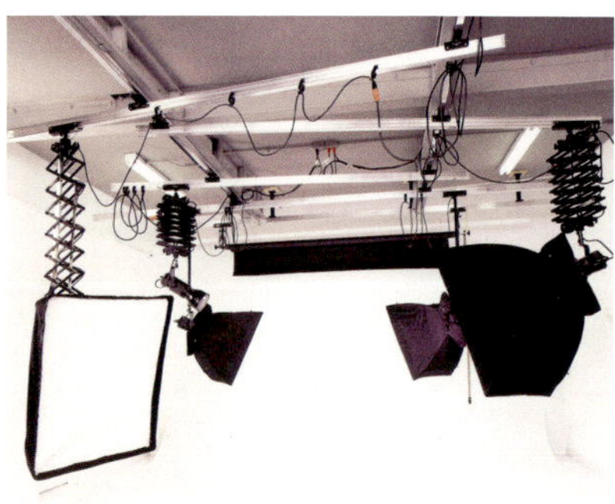

Studio set-ups range from the simple and inexpensive to the sophisticated and costly.

## What are the advantages and disadvantages of studio flash?

The following table outlines the main advantages and disadvantages of studio flash:

| Advantages | Disadvantages |
|---|---|
| Versatile, with a wide range of lighting-effects accessories | Often more expensive than equivalent continuous-source lighting systems |
| Cool-running - can be left switched on for long periods of time without overheating | More difficult to learn how to use them to their full potential |
| Balanced to natural daylight | Modelling light gives an idea of the lighting effect but the actual flash exposure may vary the final effects |
| High-powered, giving greater flexibility in setting lens aperture for exposures | |

**How do I choose a studio lighting system?**

As with buying a camera the important factor is deciding exactly what you want to achieve and then, based on your studio environment, considering what equipment is necessary to achieve it.
For example, there is little point in buying a super high-powered flash unit if you have a tiny studio.

When choosing a studio lighting system you need to consider first the flash heads and then which attachments you will need. This is an important factor as it is the attachments that actually manage the quality of light that falls on the subject.

When choosing flash heads there are several factors to consider:

Power - the greater the power of the flash head the more flexibility you will have in setting lens aperture, resulting in greater control over depth of field. However, power is relative and should be considered in relation to the size of your studio environment. You can assess the suitability, relating to power, of a head by using the formula for manual flash exposure (see page 120). For example: A flash head with a guide number of 38 (m/ISO 100) is £150/$300 and a more powerful head with a guide number of 80 (m/ISO 100) is £250/$500. Which is the better flash head to buy?

Let's assume your studio is 5 metres (15 feet) long. With an average lens aperture of f/8 the more expensive flash head has coverage of 10 metres (32 feet) - 80(GN)/8(f/stop) = 10m(FSD) - double what you need. This would give you the flexibility to shoot at apertures between the maximum opening and f/16.
The lower-priced, less powerful unit has coverage of 4.75 metres (15 feet), just about enough for the size of the studio but only at apertures up to f/8.

In this example, then, the more flexible option would be the more expensive unit. However, other factors come into play:

Ease of use - many of us have a very expensive DVD player at home although would probably admit to knowing nothing about how to use more than 10% of its functions. Arguably money has been wasted on features that are not needed or perhaps not understood.
The same can be said for lighting systems. You're better off with a system you know how to operate than one that won't do what you want it to because the control system is overly complicated.

Versatility - buy a system with the future in mind, one that offers good system back-up and a range of usable attachments and one you can expand as your skills and vision grow.

Reliability - if you intend to use your studio lighting in a professional capacity then be sure you buy a reputable and reliable brand.

**See also**

*Choosing a portable flash unit (page 108)*
*Studio lighting accessories (page 134)*

# CONTINUOUS-SOURCE LIGHTING

**See also**

*Artificial light (page 104)*

### What is continuous-source studio lighting?

Rather than emit a flash of light at the point of exposure, continuous-source lighting is always on and takes the form of tungsten or fluorescent lighting. Continuous-source lighting is often (wrongly) considered as the poor man's studio lighting. In actuality there are advantages to using continuous-source lighting in certain situations (see table opposite).

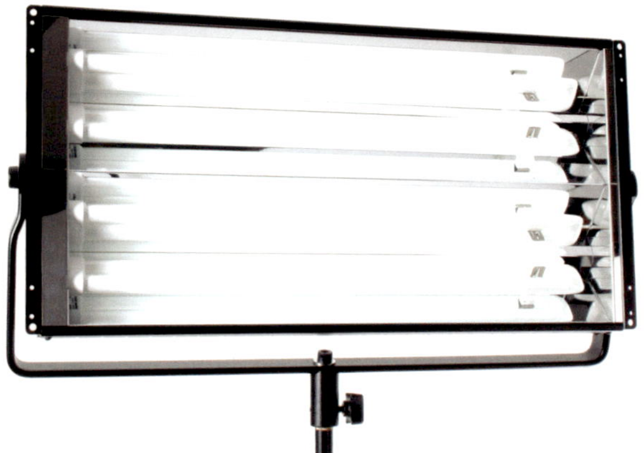

This is an example of a fluorescent continuous-source lighting unit that would be used in a studio.

### What is the difference between tungsten and fluorescent lighting?

Both are continuous light sources. Tungsten light is similar to the lighting used in most household rooms, while fluorescent lighting works on the same principle as the strip lighting you often find used in kitchens. One of the main differences is the colour temperature of the different sources.

Tungsten lighting has a colour temperature similar to daylight at sunset, which when used in conjunction with daylight-balanced film will produce an orange cast. Using tungsten-balanced film, or setting the appropriate White Balance setting on a digital camera can overcome this.

The colour temperature of fluorescent lighting is slightly cooler than that of tungsten but warmer than daylight and so too produces a colour cast when used with daylight-balanced film - this time the cast is green. Using optical colour correction filters will overcome this cast, although different films react in different ways and so some experimentation will be required. Again, there is a specific fluorescent WB setting on digital cameras.

### What are hot lights?

Hot lights are a form of tungsten lighting that run very hot. They may be used with varying strength of bulb from 500W Photopearl (around 10 times more powerful than an ordinary household light bulb) to 275W and 500W Photofloods, which are the equivalent of 8 and 16 100W household light bulbs, respectively.

Using them in conjunction with a reflector can alter the quality of their light, although care should be taken to avoid the heat from the bulbs setting fire to the reflector. Another disadvantage of hot lights is the closeness at which they need to be used, which can cause discomfort to models during long sittings.

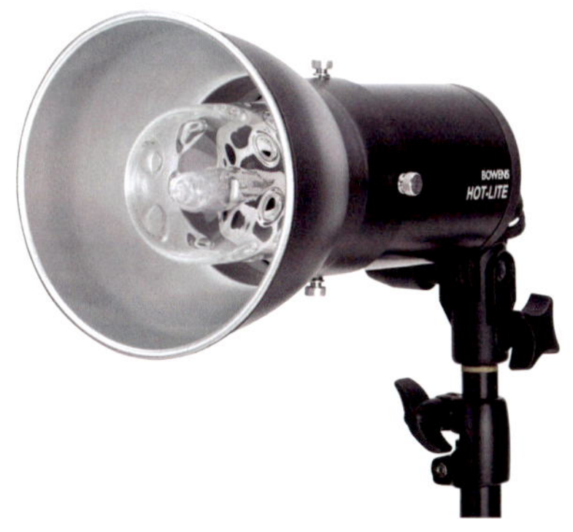


Hot lights are another form of continuous-source studio lighting.

### What are the advantages and disadvantages of continuous-source lighting?

The advantages and disadvantages of continuous-source lighting are given in the following table:

| Lighting type | Advantages | Disadvantages |
|---|---|---|
| Professional tungsten lights | Ideal for specialist applications | Low intensity often dictates use of wide apertures only |
| | What you see is what you get (WYSIWYG) lighting | Single-function makes them less flexible than flash |
| | | Can be expensive compared to alternative options |
| Low-cost hot lights | Relatively low entry cost | Low-powered |
| | Simple to use | Hot-running and inclined to overheat |
| | What you see is what you get (WYSIWYG) lighting | Need to be properly balanced with CC filters if used with daylight-balanced film |
| Fluorescent lighting | Easy to use, ideal for beginners | Need to be properly balanced with CC filters if used with daylight-balanced film |
| | Cool-running and less liable to overheating. Also more comfortable for a model | Cannot be mixed with flash lighting |
| | Newer models have largely overcome the shortcomings of older versions | Practically, can only be used as a soft light source |
| | | Flickering can cause poor effects in the final image |

# STUDIO LIGHTING ACCESSORIES

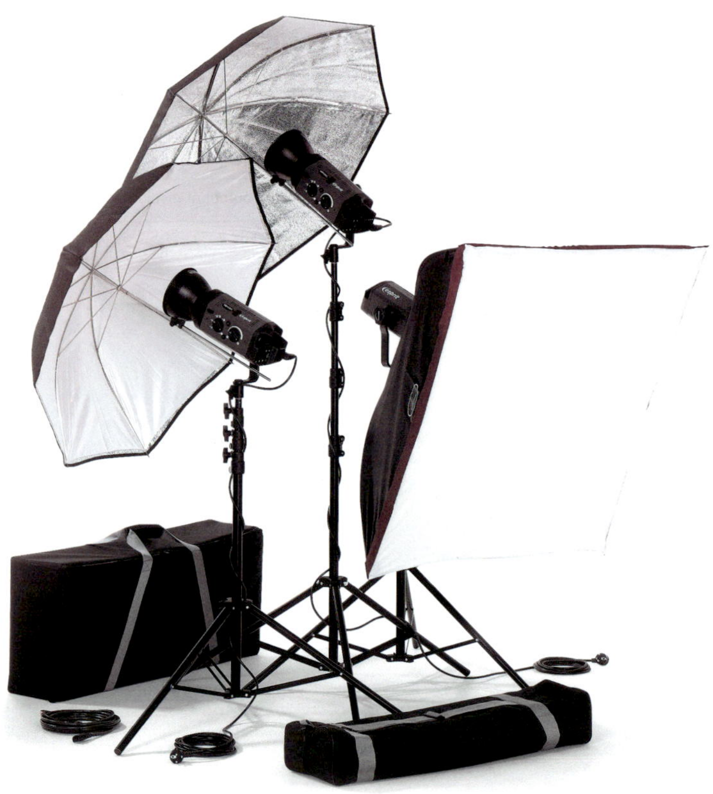

Lighting accessories range from the simple to the complex. Each changes the way light falls on the subject and can be used for creative as well as technical effect.

## What lighting accessories are available?

There is a multitude of lighting accessories available with studio flash systems, from various types of reflector, umbrellas, diffusers and lighting-direction aids. Many of these accessories have specific uses, as described in the following pages.

## What are the most commonly used accessories?

General accessories tend to be more commonly used, as they can be applied in a variety of different scenarios. For example, soft boxes will change the quality of a flash's light from hard to soft. Similarly umbrellas are often used to bounce light, so altering its quality. General-purpose reflectors give an even coverage and high light output, with medium-quality lighting. Other accessory types, such as snoots, tend to be used for more specific applications.

### When would I use a reflector?

Studio lighting reflectors, which are also referred to as dish reflectors (because of their shape) attach to the front of the flash head and produce hard directional light. There are several types of reflector, as outlined in the following table:

| Reflector type | Effect |
|---|---|
| General-purpose | Give an even coverage and high light output of medium to high contrast (quality). |
| Wide-angle | Also known as spill-kill reflectors. Create a very broad, even light. Designed for use with umbrellas to complement and enhance the performance of the umbrella. Produce hard-quality lighting. |
| Key-light | Have highly polished surfaces increasing brightness by around 1 to 2 stops. However, the light is contrast-rich (hard quality) with high specularity. |
| High-performance | Designed to maximise light output and particularly good for use when bouncing light off ceilings or walls. Produce a softer light quality. |
| Grid | Create controlled pools of light each with narrow coverage but without loss in intensity. Typically high-contrast lighting with minimal fall-off. |
| Soft-light | Similar in a way to a soft box, soft lights produce broad, even light coverage that is soft in quality. Ideal for fashion and glamour work. |
| Sunlight | Designed to replicate sunlight with a broad beam of light and high output levels. Higher in contrast than a soft light, they are ideal for photographing architectural models. |
| Ring light | Highly distinctive lighting often used in portrait photography. Can appear flat if used ineffectively. |
| Backlight | Produce a natural oval vignette that is ideally suited to illuminating backgrounds in portrait photography. |

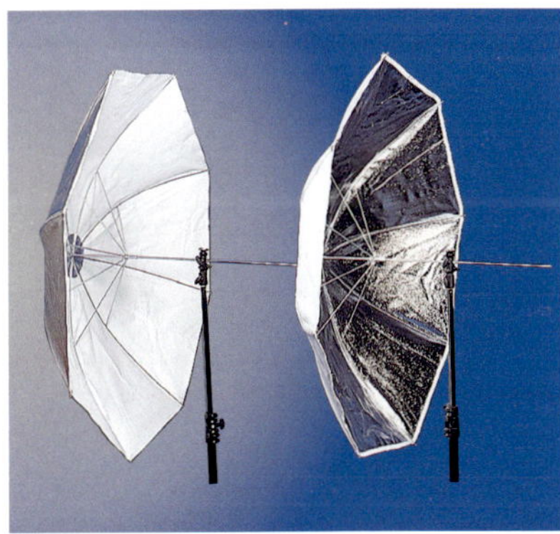

Umbrellas are used to create omni-directional, diffused lighting from a direct point source (the flash unit).

### When would I use an umbrella?

Perhaps the most commonly used accessory in the studio, umbrellas can operate as either a reflector, when light is bounced off it, or as a diffuser, when light is shone through it. They are inexpensive and versatile, making them an ideal start-up accessory.

As well as different sizes, umbrellas come in varying colours, typically white, silver or gold (or a combination of two colours, one on either side). Colour affects the quality of light. White - the most popular colour - produces soft, non-directional lighting. Metallic (silver and gold) umbrellas produce much harder-quality light that is more directional. Additionally gold umbrellas produce lighting warmer in colour temperature.

### What is the purpose of a soft box?

Soft boxes produce an even spread of soft, diffused light, much like sunlight on a cloudy day. They are available in different sizes; the larger the box the softer the quality of the light, depending on their position relative to the subject. They are ideal for use in fashion, glamour and portrait photography.

**Tip**

*Better-quality soft boxes are made with an internal translucent diffuser that sits between the light source and the external material to produce an even distribution of light across the whole surface of the box. This can be critical when using particularly large boxes.*

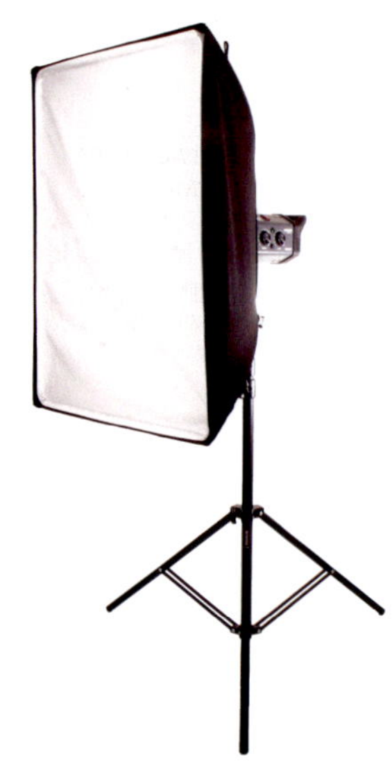

A soft box creates soft, diffused lighting.

### What are barn doors?

Barn doors limit light spill in areas where illumination isn't required. Constructed of two or, more usually, four-hinged 'doors' or flaps, each flap can be moved to concentrate light into specific areas only. When all four doors are folded in close together they act as a funnel - much like a snoot.

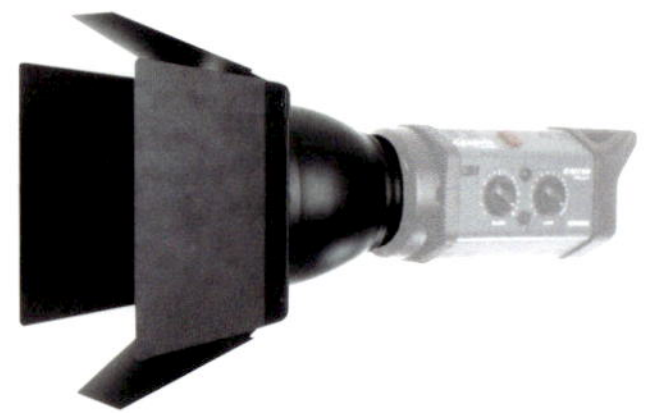

Barn doors enable highly controlled directional lighting.

### What's a snoot?

Snoots funnel light into a tight beam that is typically used to highlight key features of a subject, such as a model's eyes or hair. They are usually used as an accessory to a second light, to complement a main light. Snoots will reduce the brightness of the flash head by around 2 stops.

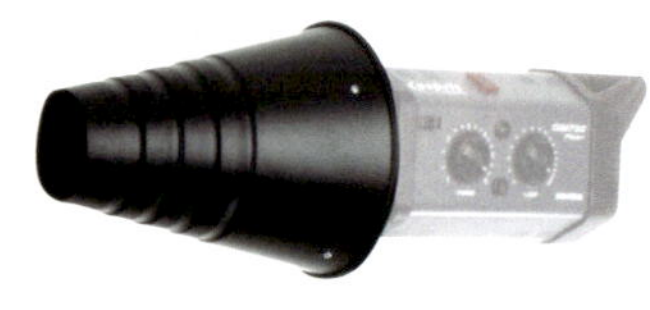

A snoot directs a pin-point source of light on to the subject.

## What are lighting ratios?

Lighting ratios refer to the level of contrast and are a measure of the difference in stops between the brightness of the shadow areas compared to the highlights. For example, say you have a model lit on her left side by a direct light and on her right side by a soft light. If the direct light is twice as bright as the soft light then the lighting ratio is 2:1. By using lighting ratios you can determine how contrast will appear in the final image.

Lighting ratios

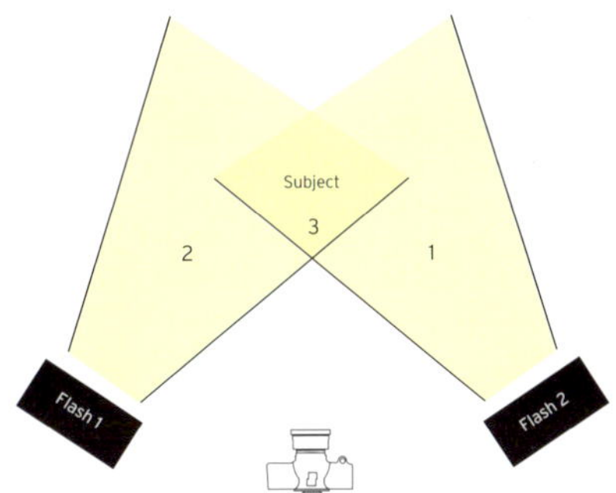


Lighting ratios are important when calculating flash exposures.

## How do I measure lighting ratios?

To measure the lighting ratio (in this instance for a two-unit set-up), first take a flash meter reading from the secondary light (having turned off the main light). Then take a reading from the main light with the secondary light switched off. Now switch on both lights and take a flash meter reading from the position where the light from the two lights overlap. The difference in EV between the secondary light (the first reading) and the combined lighting (the last reading) will give you your ratio.

For example, say the first reading gave an aperture of f/4 and the second reading gave an aperture of f/8. The lighting ratio for the primary and secondary lights is 2:1. Now let's say the final (combined) reading gave an aperture of f/11 - the lighting ratio for the whole scene is 3:1.

## Why do I need to understand lighting ratios?

Knowing the lighting ratio will firstly tell you whether the brightness range falls within the latitude of the film or sensor used. For example, if the ratio is 6:1 and film latitude is only 5 stops then detail will be lost from the scene in either the brightest or darkest stop of light, depending on the exposure.

Additionally, knowing the lighting ratio will help you visualise exactly the strength of shadows in the final image, more so than the use of modelling lights.

## What is meant by the term 'spatial relationships'?

In relation to studio photography the term 'spatial relationship' refers to the visual relationship between the subject and the background. The primary consideration is whether the background forms part of the scene, in which case it needs to appear in focus, or whether it is to be excluded from forming an integral part of the scene, in which case it needs to appear out of focus.

### How do I control spatial relationships?

Depth of field controls how the background appears in relation to the subject. By blurring the background, emphasis is placed on the subject, while a wide depth of field will lend equal weight to subject and background objects. Depth of field is controlled, in part, by lens aperture, hence the importance of having flexibility in setting lens apertures.

A small aperture, such as f/11 or f/16, will increase depth of field, making background objects appear sharper. Conversely, a large aperture minimises depth of field, blurring background objects and de-emphasising their importance in the picture space.

### Tip

*Depth of field is also affected by focal length and camera-to-subject distance. Long focal length lenses reduce depth of field and short focal length (wide-angle) lenses increase it. Also depth of field reduces with shorter camera-to-subject distances.*

### See also

*Positioning the flash unit (page 116)*

### What is the importance of the angle of light?

Humans are used to lighting that falls on a subject from an angle between 0 and 180 degrees on the lateral axis (i.e. from the sun as it rises and falls). Natural light never comes from an angle beyond 180 degrees, i.e. from below. When lighting a subject in a studio, if you are trying to create an impression of natural light then it is important to mirror the angle of light of the sun. On the horizontal axis, avoiding head-on lighting will help to accentuate form and reduce the likelihood of red-eye.

### See also

*Inverse Square Law (page 23)*
*Direction of light (page 28)*

### Where should studio lights be positioned in relation to the subject?

A common mistake made by novices is to position the lights too far from the subject. If the lights are set too far away then flexibility in selecting lens apertures is reduced because of light fall off, as per the Inverse Square Law. Moving the lights closer to the subject will have the effect of producing softer all-round light and greater exposure flexibility.

In terms of angle-to-subject the position of the lights will affect shadow and contrast. Straight on to the subject and few, if any, shadows will form, creating a flat image lacking any form. As you move the lights towards 90 degrees to the subject (on the horizontal axis), shadows will lengthen. The ideal angle tends to be between 30 and 45 degrees to the subject. Placing the lights behind the subject will create rim lighting.

### What options do I have with a single-light set-up?

It is important to understand that in any scene one light acts as the primary source, providing the energy in the photograph. It is the primary light that sets the direction, character and strength of the scene lighting, with all other lights working off the main light. Mastering the key light is essential to good studio photography and starting out with a one-unit set-up will help you hone this skill.

A single light is best used in conjunction with a reflector or with natural fill-in light from a window or doorway. Position the flash unit at an angle between 30 and 45 degrees to the subject and place the reflector directly opposite the flash, close to the subject (but out of the picture). Alternatively, place the subject so he or she is side-on to the natural light source, which should be on the opposite side to the flash unit. To soften light from the flash unit, use a soft-box, umbrella or soft reflector.

Single-light set-up

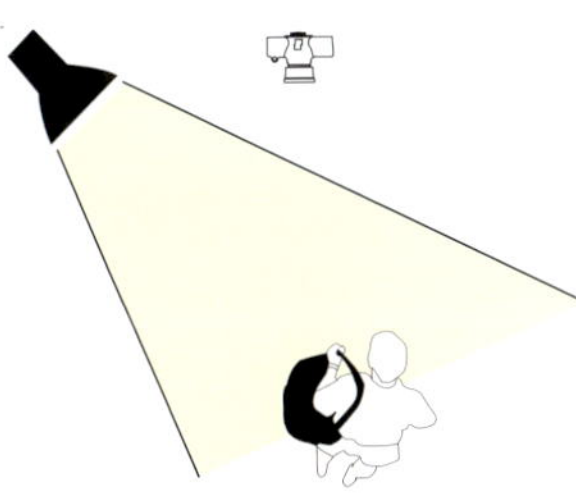

A single-light set-up (above) can be highly effective. Adding a reflector to redirect light back into the shadow areas, lifting the shadows, can also work effectively.

A three-light set-up (right) adds even more flexibility and also complexity. A third light can be used to add to the creative options or simply as a background light. The options are endless.

### What options do I have with a two-light set-up?

Adding a second light will increase creative options and add some flexibility. However, remember that one light will remain the key light and the additional, second light needs to work in harmony with the primary light.

Two-light set-up

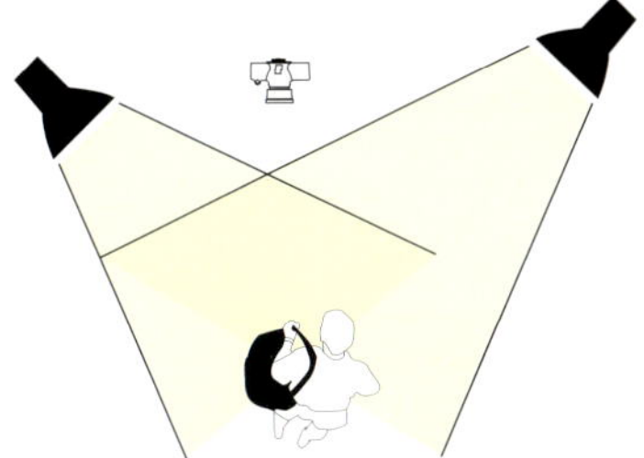

Two-light set-ups increase your lighting options. Typically one light will always be the primary source, with the second light used as a fill light or for creative effect.

### What options do I have with a three-light set-up?

Adding a third light further increases creative options and flexibility, but also adds to complexity - sometimes unnecessarily. In the examples, notice that the original key light remains the primary light and the second and third lights are complementing its effects.

Three-light set-up

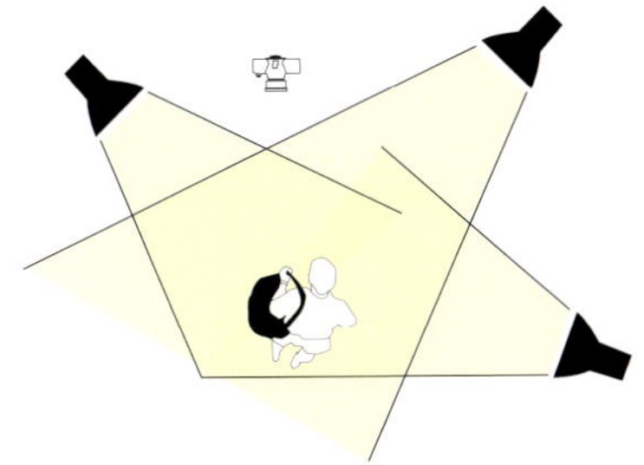

## ACKNOWLEDGEMENTS

Thank you to the following people who helped in the production of this book:

Brian Morris, Lucy Bryan and Sanaz Nazemi at AVA Publishing; David Crow, Amy Morgan, Peter Cope, Susan Czarnecki, Mary-Ann D'cruz, Richard Williams and Indexing Specialists (UK) Ltd.

Finally, thanks to my family, who always put up with the most.

## CREDITS

Pages 22 and 23: Images courtesy of Jorge Coimbra (www.jorgecoimbra.home.sapo.pt)
Pages 26, 27, 42, 46, 47, 66, 67 and 126: Images courtesy of Peter Cope
Pages 28, 37, 103 and 125: Images courtesy of Simon Stafford © Simon Stafford (www.simonstafford.co.uk)
Pages 41, 64 (top), 70, 106 (bottom) and 111: Images courtesy of Intro 2020 Ltd UK
Page 49: Image courtesy of Lastolite
Pages 50 and 52: Images courtesy of Susan Czarnecki
Page 55: Images courtesy of Brian Morris
Page 71: Image courtesy of Neda Taleban at Scarlet Rose Photography
Pages 82 and 104: Images courtesy of Heather McFarland (www.hkmphotos.com)
Pages 85, 87, 88, 89, 92, 93 and 95: Images courtesy of Dr Andrew Stevens
Pages 87, 107 and 113: Images supplied courtesy of Nikon Corporation
Page 90: Image courtesy of Marion Luijten (www.marionluijtenphotography.com)
Page 94: Image courtesy of Mark Plonsky (www.mplonsky.com/photo)
Page 96: Image courtesy of Jasmine Studios (www.jasminestudios.com)
Pages 106 (top), 132, 133 and 136: © photographs courtesy of Bowens International Ltd 2007
Page 112: Images courtesy of Speed Graphic Mail Order Ltd
Page 114: Images courtesy of John Clements
Page 117: Image courtesy of Nina Andersen (www.eyesondesign.net)
Page 122: Image courtesy of John Robinson
Page 123: Fuji Velvia 100 daylight colour transparency film, courtesy of Fujifilm